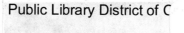

HMMMMTH

OOOWWWW!

WHAT'S THE MATTER, SON?

DID YOU HAVE A BAD DREAM?

HE'S NOT A BABY ANYMORE, DEAR. DON'T SMOTHER HIM.

HE'LL ALWAYS BE MY BABY. WHAT'S THE MATTER, LYNDON?

MY KNEE, IT HURTS!

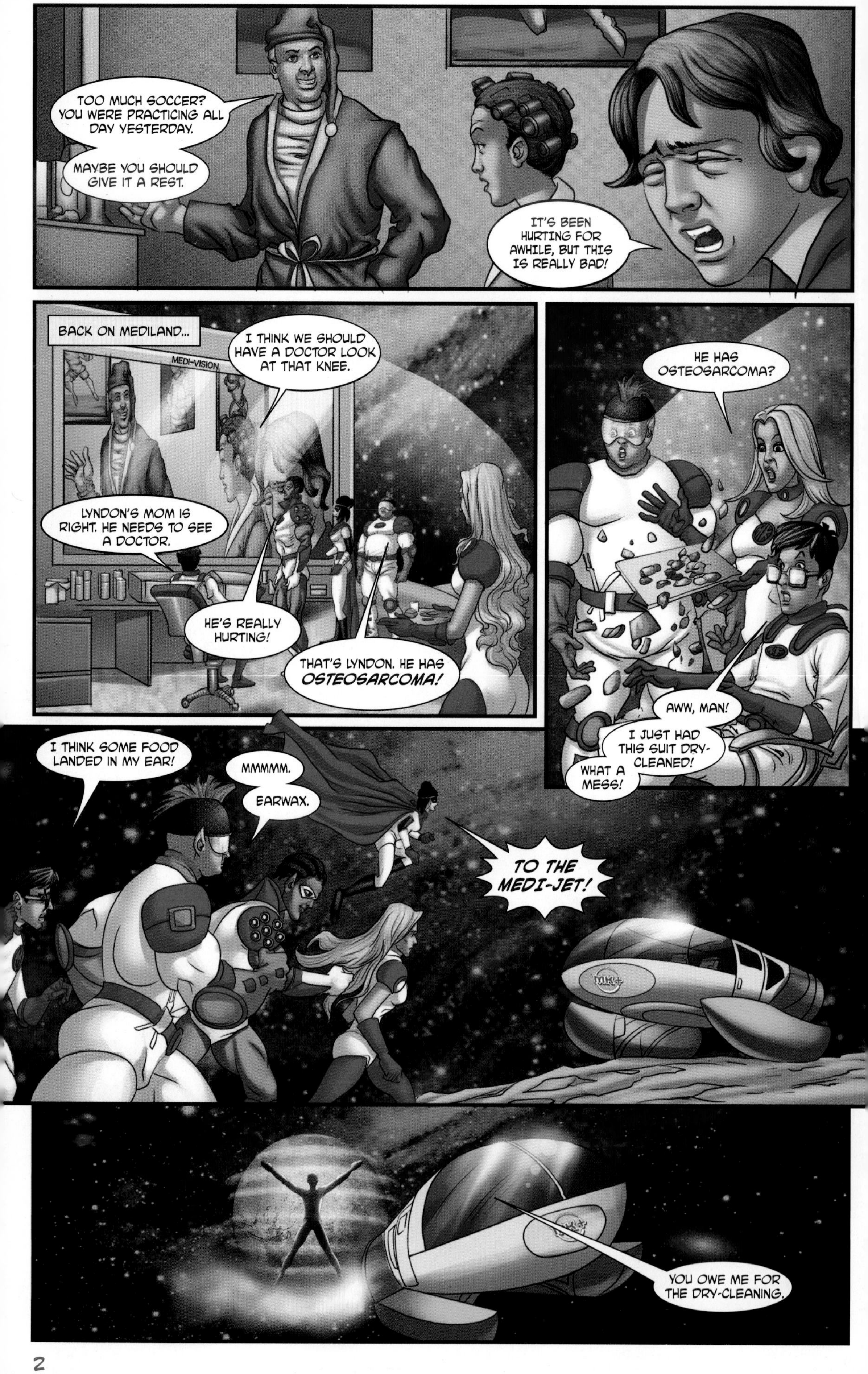
TOO MUCH SOCCER? YOU WERE PRACTICING ALL DAY YESTERDAY.
MAYBE YOU SHOULD GIVE IT A REST.
IT'S BEEN HURTING FOR AWHILE, BUT THIS IS REALLY BAD!
BACK ON MEDILAND...
MEDI-VISION
I THINK WE SHOULD HAVE A DOCTOR LOOK AT THAT KNEE.
LYNDON'S MOM IS RIGHT. HE NEEDS TO SEE A DOCTOR.
HE'S REALLY HURTING!
THAT'S LYNDON. HE HAS OSTEOSARCOMA!
HE HAS OSTEOSARCOMA?
AWW, MAN!
I JUST HAD THIS SUIT DRY-CLEANED!
WHAT A MESS!
I THINK SOME FOOD LANDED IN MY EAR!
MMMMM.
EARWAX.
TO THE MEDI-JET!
YOU OWE ME FOR THE DRY-CLEANING.

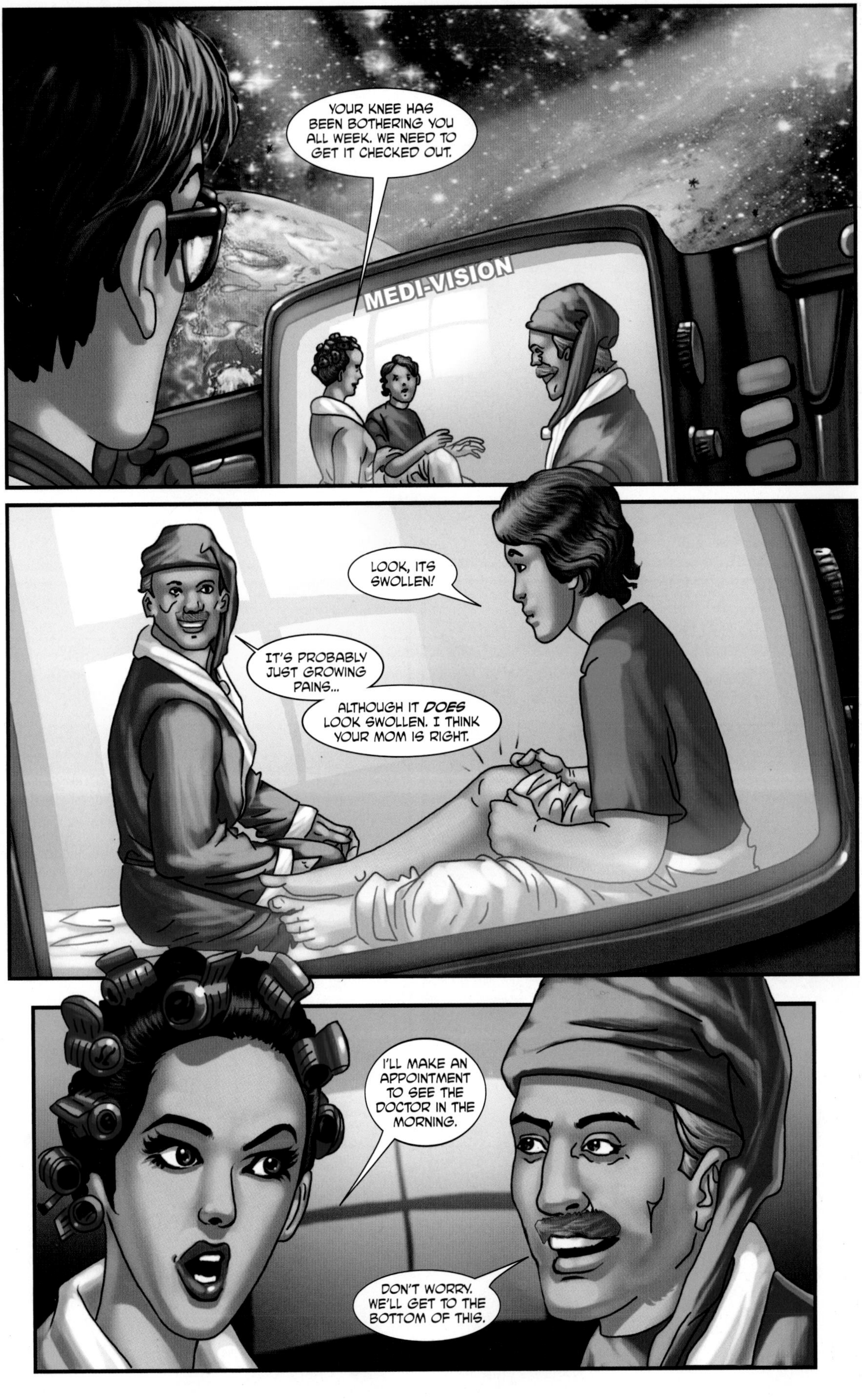
YOUR KNEE HAS BEEN BOTHERING YOU ALL WEEK. WE NEED TO GET IT CHECKED OUT.
MEDI-VISION
LOOK, ITS SWOLLEN!
IT'S PROBABLY JUST GROWING PAINS...
ALTHOUGH IT *DOES* LOOK SWOLLEN. I THINK YOUR MOM IS RIGHT.
I'LL MAKE AN APPOINTMENT TO SEE THE DOCTOR IN THE MORNING.
DON'T WORRY. WE'LL GET TO THE BOTTOM OF THIS.

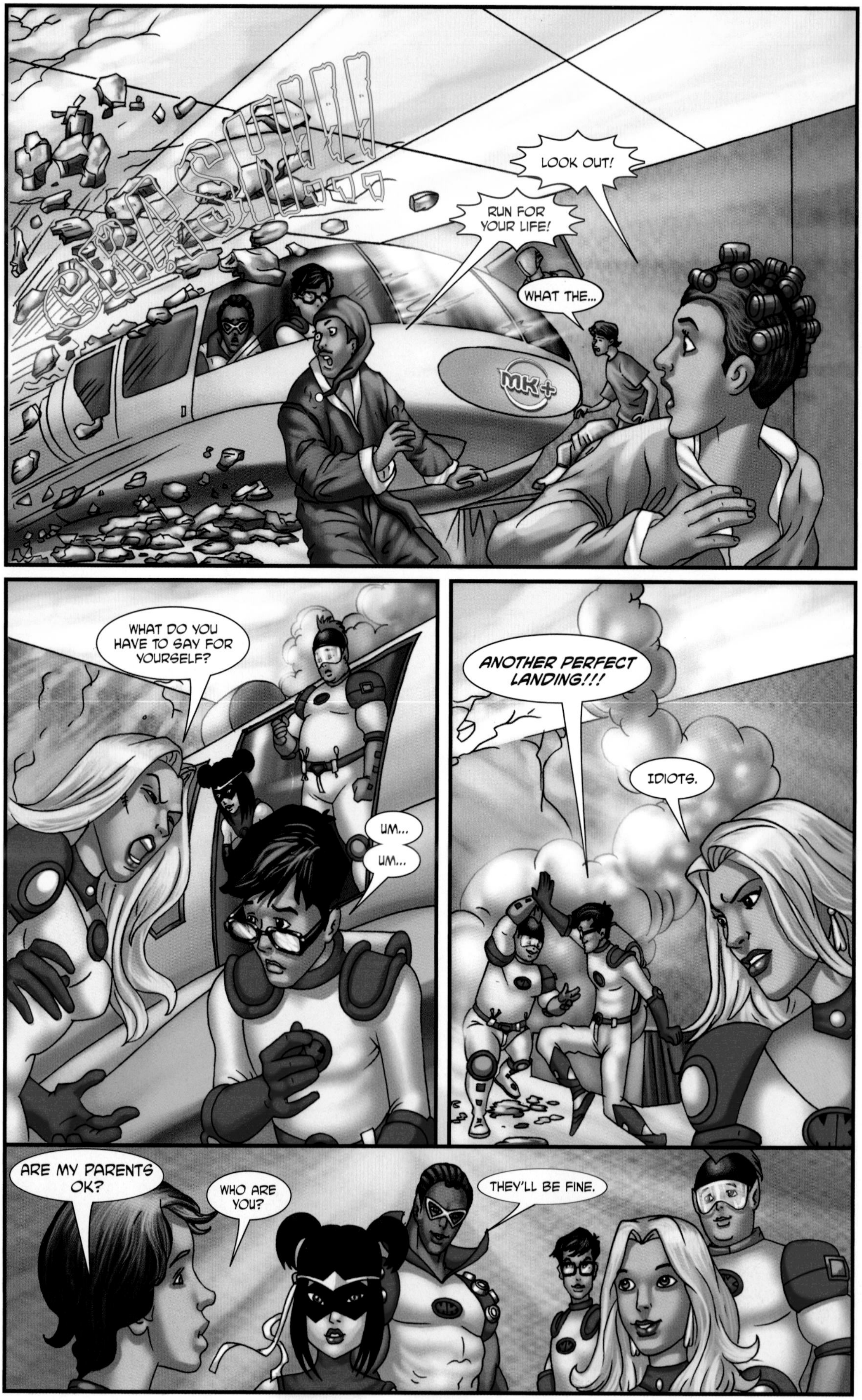
CRASH!!!!
LOOK OUT!
RUN FOR YOUR LIFE!
WHAT THE...
WHAT DO YOU HAVE TO SAY FOR YOURSELF?
UM...
UM...
ANOTHER PERFECT LANDING!!!
IDIOTS.
ARE MY PARENTS OK?
WHO ARE YOU?
THEY'LL BE FINE.

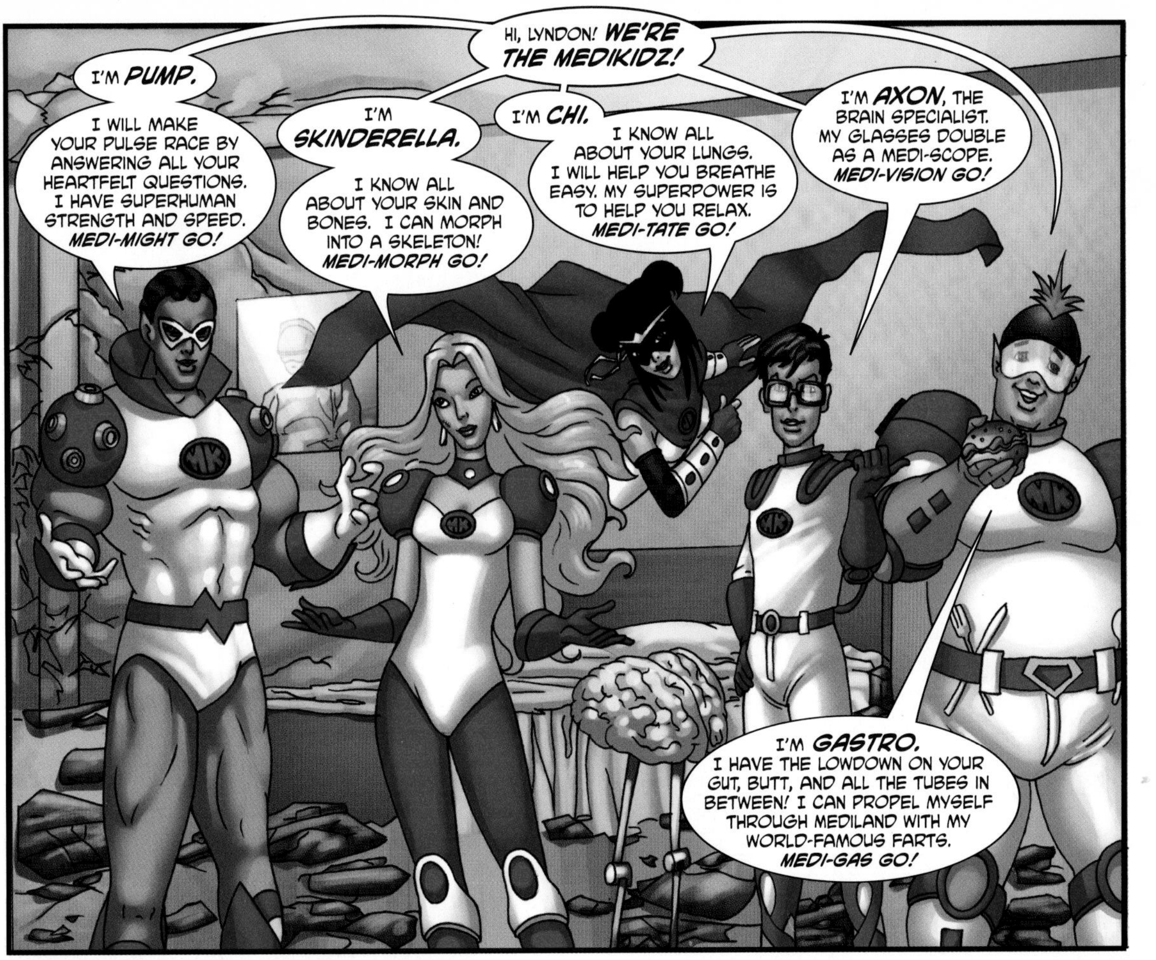
HI, LYNDON! WE'RE THE MEDIKIDZ!
I'M PUMP.
I WILL MAKE YOUR PULSE RACE BY ANSWERING ALL YOUR HEARTFELT QUESTIONS. I HAVE SUPERHUMAN STRENGTH AND SPEED. MEDI-MIGHT GO!
I'M SKINDERELLA.
I KNOW ALL ABOUT YOUR SKIN AND BONES. I CAN MORPH INTO A SKELETON! MEDI-MORPH GO!
I'M CHI.
I KNOW ALL ABOUT YOUR LUNGS. I WILL HELP YOU BREATHE EASY. MY SUPERPOWER IS TO HELP YOU RELAX. MEDI-TATE GO!
I'M AXON, THE BRAIN SPECIALIST. MY GLASSES DOUBLE AS A MEDI-SCOPE. MEDI-VISION GO!
I'M GASTRO. I HAVE THE LOWDOWN ON YOUR GUT, BUTT, AND ALL THE TUBES IN BETWEEN! I CAN PROPEL MYSELF THROUGH MEDILAND WITH MY WORLD-FAMOUS FARTS. MEDI-GAS GO!

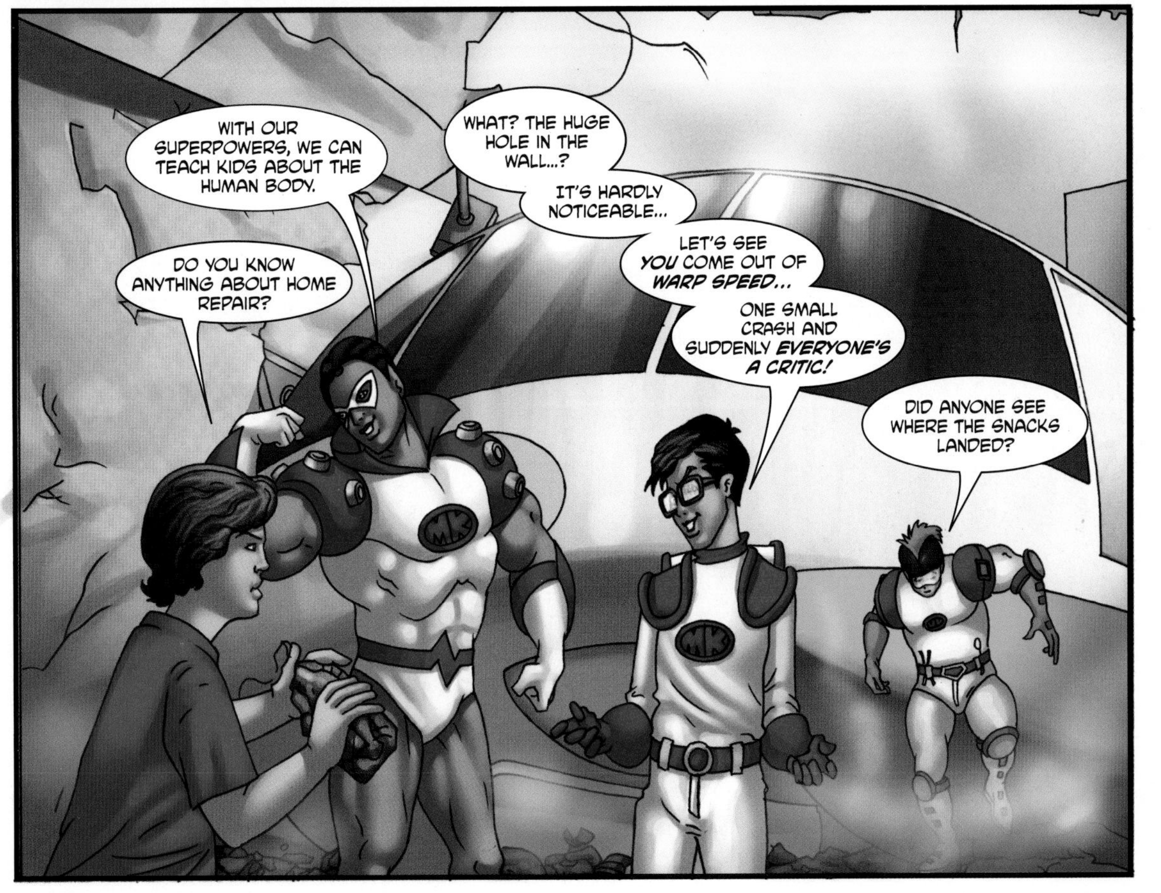
WITH OUR SUPERPOWERS, WE CAN TEACH KIDS ABOUT THE HUMAN BODY.
DO YOU KNOW ANYTHING ABOUT HOME REPAIR?
WHAT? THE HUGE HOLE IN THE WALL...?
IT'S HARDLY NOTICEABLE...
LET'S SEE YOU COME OUT OF WARP SPEED...
ONE SMALL CRASH AND SUDDENLY EVERYONE'S A CRITIC!
DID ANYONE SEE WHERE THE SNACKS LANDED?

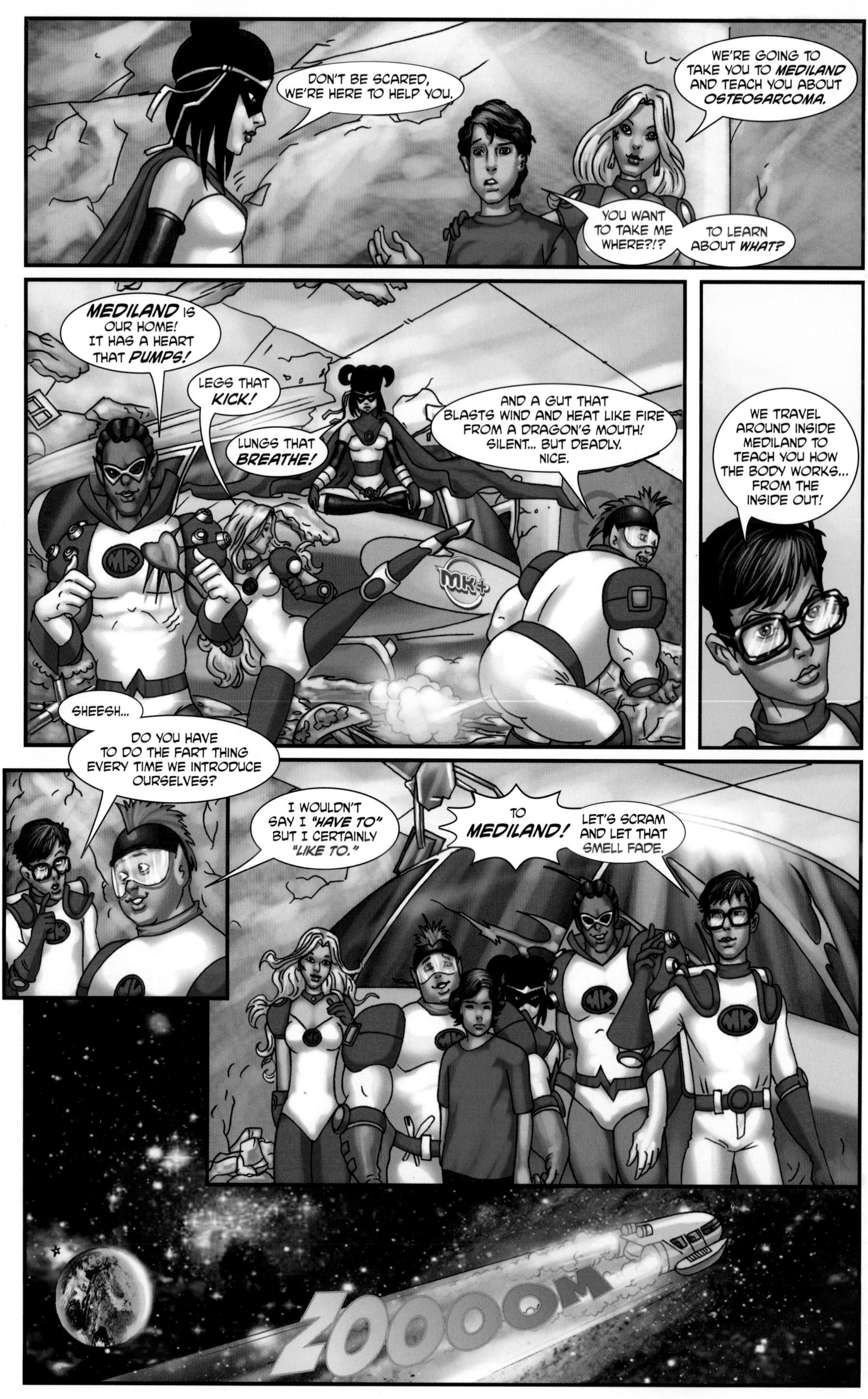
DON'T BE SCARED, WE'RE HERE TO HELP YOU.
WE'RE GOING TO TAKE YOU TO MEDILAND AND TEACH YOU ABOUT OSTEOSARCOMA.
YOU WANT TO TAKE ME WHERE?!?
TO LEARN ABOUT WHAT?
MEDILAND IS OUR HOME! IT HAS A HEART THAT PUMPS!
LEGS THAT KICK!
LUNGS THAT BREATHE!
AND A GUT THAT BLASTS WIND AND HEAT LIKE FIRE FROM A DRAGON'S MOUTH! SILENT... BUT DEADLY. NICE.
MK+
WE TRAVEL AROUND INSIDE MEDILAND TO TEACH YOU HOW THE BODY WORKS... FROM THE INSIDE OUT!
SHEESH...
DO YOU HAVE TO DO THE FART THING EVERY TIME WE INTRODUCE OURSELVES?
I WOULDN'T SAY I "HAVE TO" BUT I CERTAINLY "LIKE TO."
TO MEDILAND!
LET'S SCRAM AND LET THAT SMELL FADE.
ZOOOOM

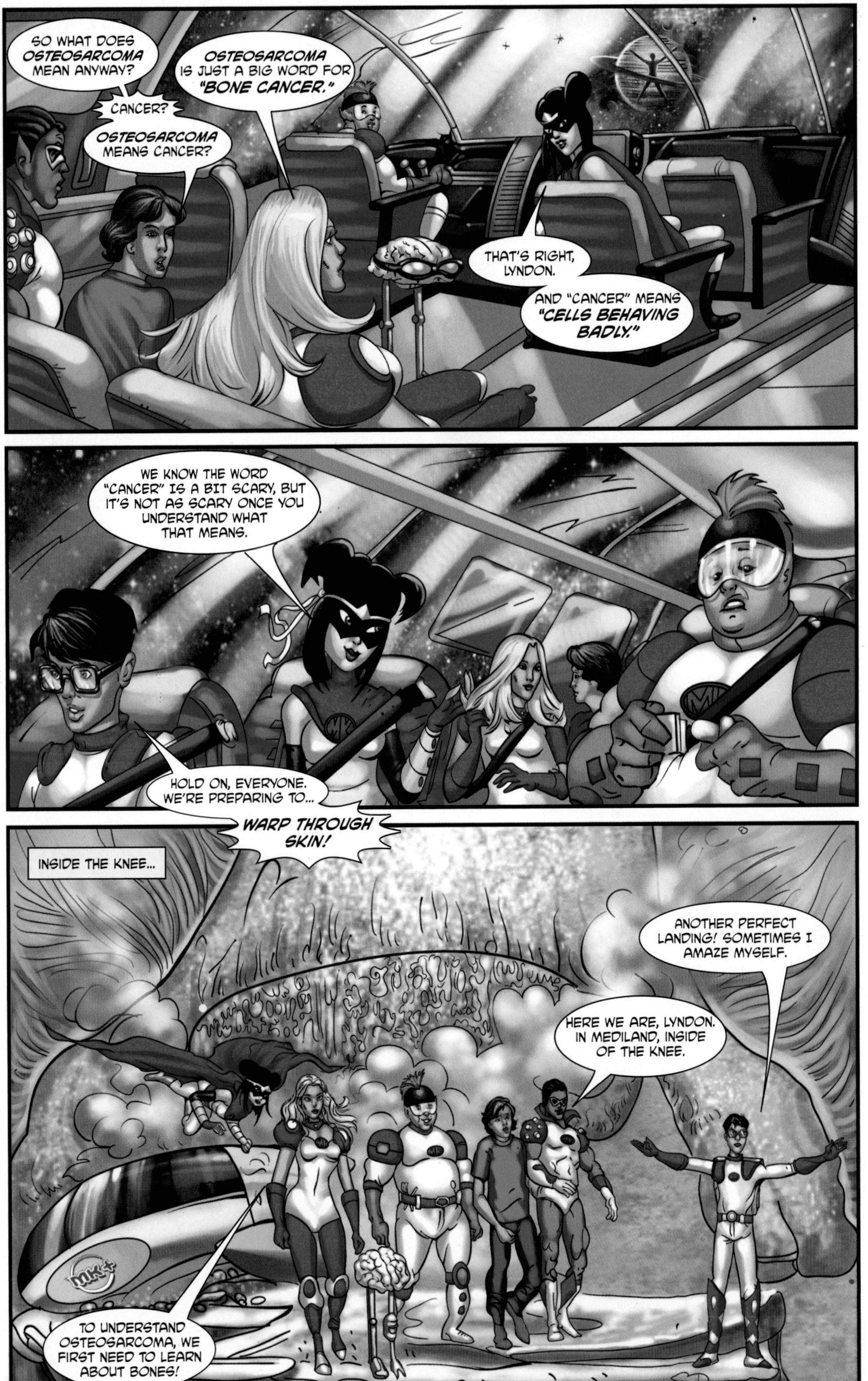
SO WHAT DOES OSTEOSARCOMA MEAN ANYWAY?
CANCER?
OSTEOSARCOMA MEANS CANCER?
OSTEOSARCOMA IS JUST A BIG WORD FOR "BONE CANCER."
THAT'S RIGHT, LYNDON.
AND "CANCER" MEANS "CELLS BEHAVING BADLY."
WE KNOW THE WORD "CANCER" IS A BIT SCARY, BUT IT'S NOT AS SCARY ONCE YOU UNDERSTAND WHAT THAT MEANS.
HOLD ON, EVERYONE. WE'RE PREPARING TO...
WARP THROUGH SKIN!
INSIDE THE KNEE...
ANOTHER PERFECT LANDING! SOMETIMES I AMAZE MYSELF.
HERE WE ARE, LYNDON. IN MEDILAND, INSIDE OF THE KNEE.
TO UNDERSTAND OSTEOSARCOMA, WE FIRST NEED TO LEARN ABOUT BONES!

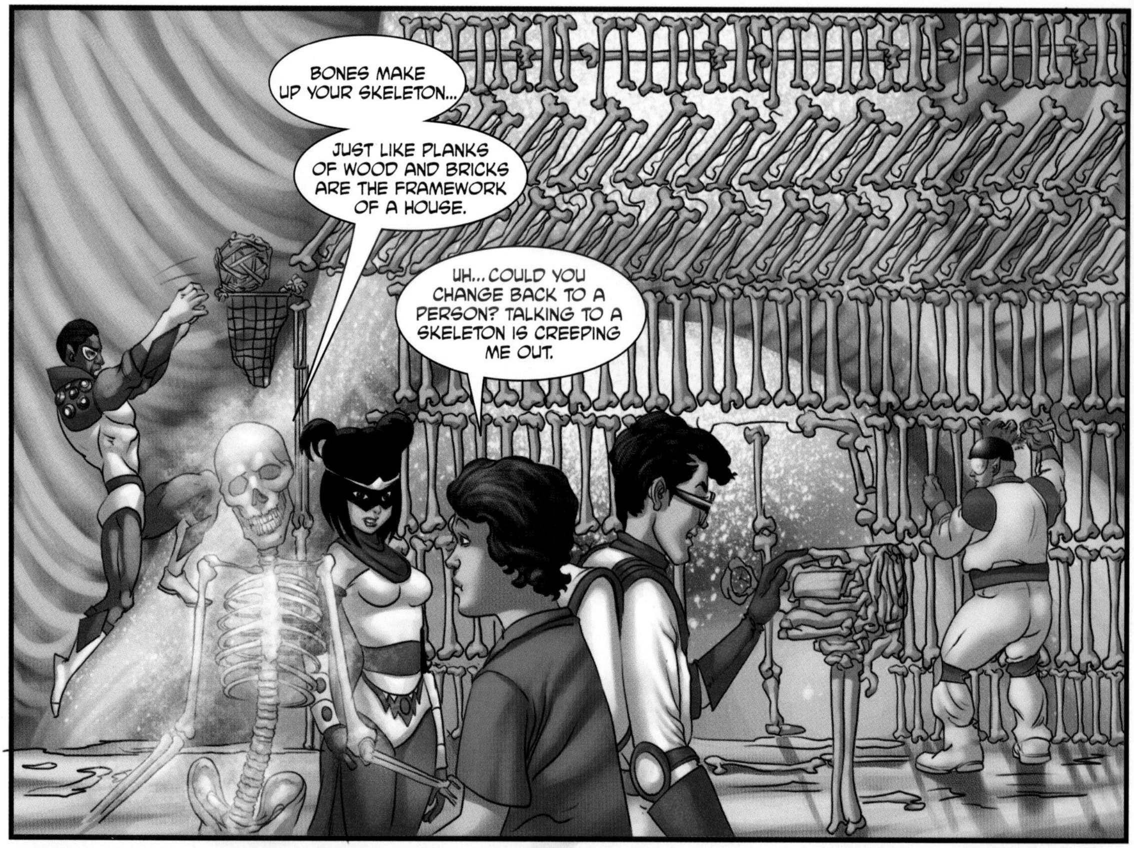
BONES MAKE UP YOUR SKELETON...
JUST LIKE PLANKS OF WOOD AND BRICKS ARE THE FRAMEWORK OF A HOUSE.
UH... COULD YOU CHANGE BACK TO A PERSON? TALKING TO A SKELETON IS CREEPING ME OUT.

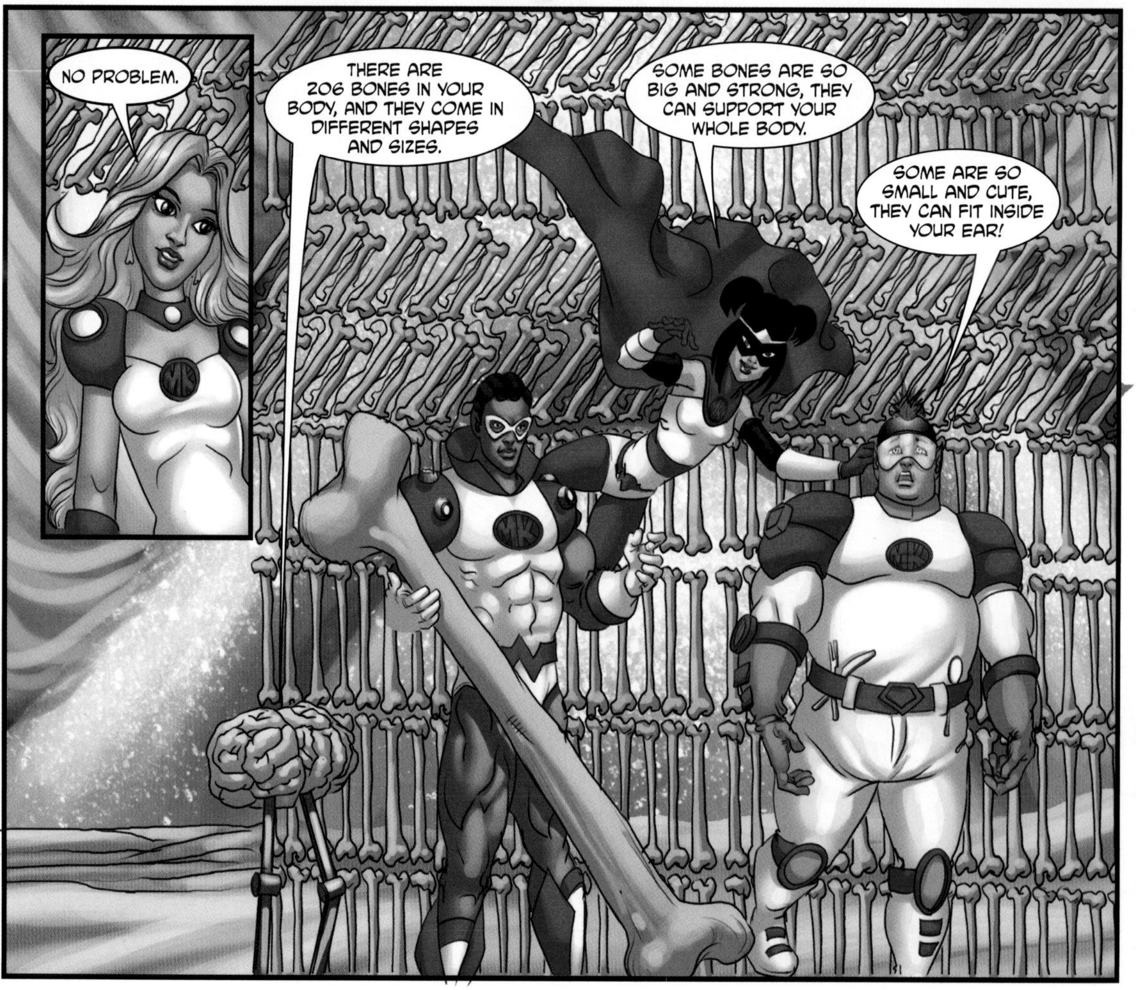
NO PROBLEM.
THERE ARE 206 BONES IN YOUR BODY, AND THEY COME IN DIFFERENT SHAPES AND SIZES.
SOME BONES ARE SO BIG AND STRONG, THEY CAN SUPPORT YOUR WHOLE BODY.
SOME ARE SO SMALL AND CUTE, THEY CAN FIT INSIDE YOUR EAR!

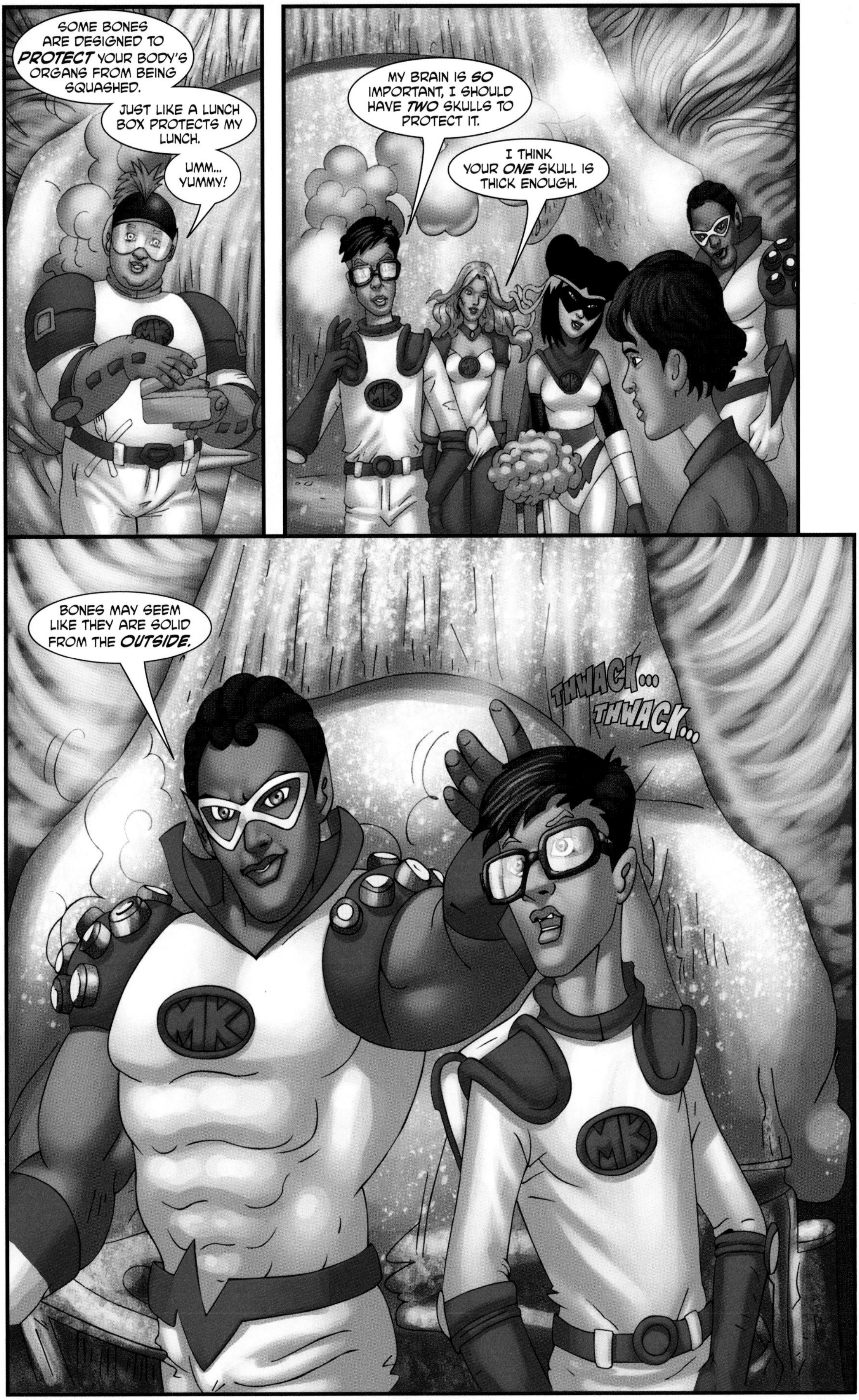
SOME BONES ARE DESIGNED TO PROTECT YOUR BODY'S ORGANS FROM BEING SQUASHED.
JUST LIKE A LUNCH BOX PROTECTS MY LUNCH.
UMM... YUMMY!
MY BRAIN IS SO IMPORTANT, I SHOULD HAVE TWO SKULLS TO PROTECT IT.
I THINK YOUR ONE SKULL IS THICK ENOUGH.
BONES MAY SEEM LIKE THEY ARE SOLID FROM THE OUTSIDE.
THWACK... THWACK...

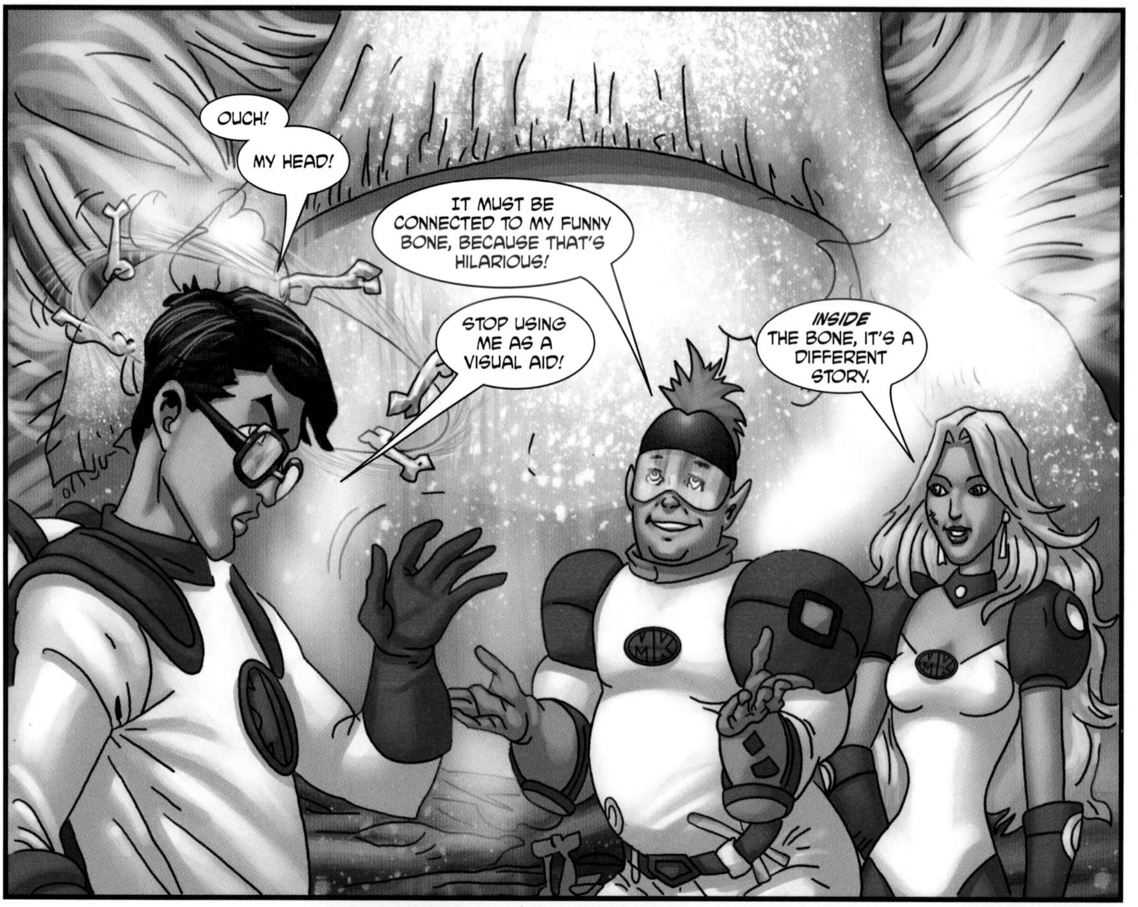
OUCH!
MY HEAD!
IT MUST BE CONNECTED TO MY FUNNY BONE, BECAUSE THAT'S HILARIOUS!
STOP USING ME AS A VISUAL AID!
INSIDE THE BONE, IT'S A DIFFERENT STORY.

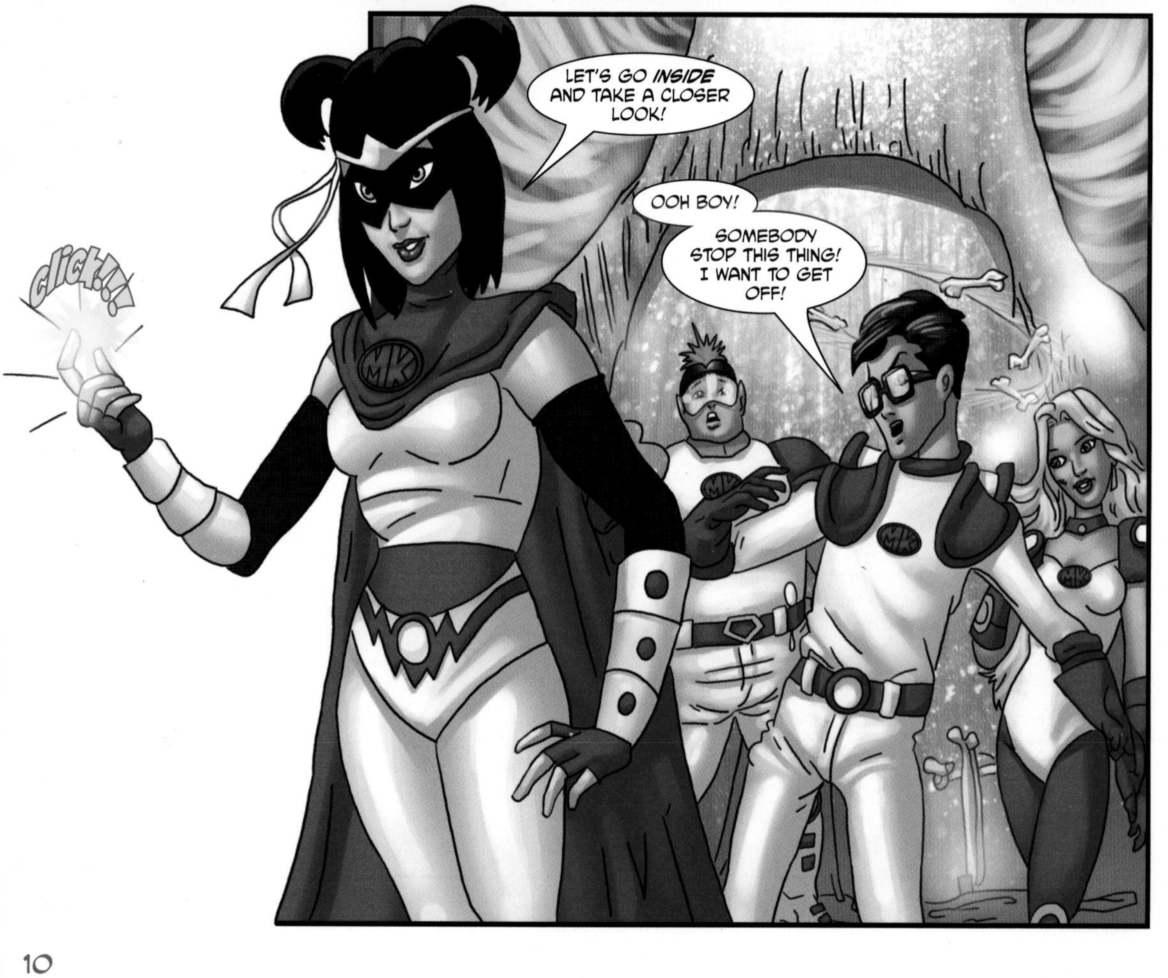
click!!!
LET'S GO *INSIDE* AND TAKE A CLOSER LOOK!
OOH BOY!
SOMEBODY STOP THIS THING! I WANT TO GET OFF!

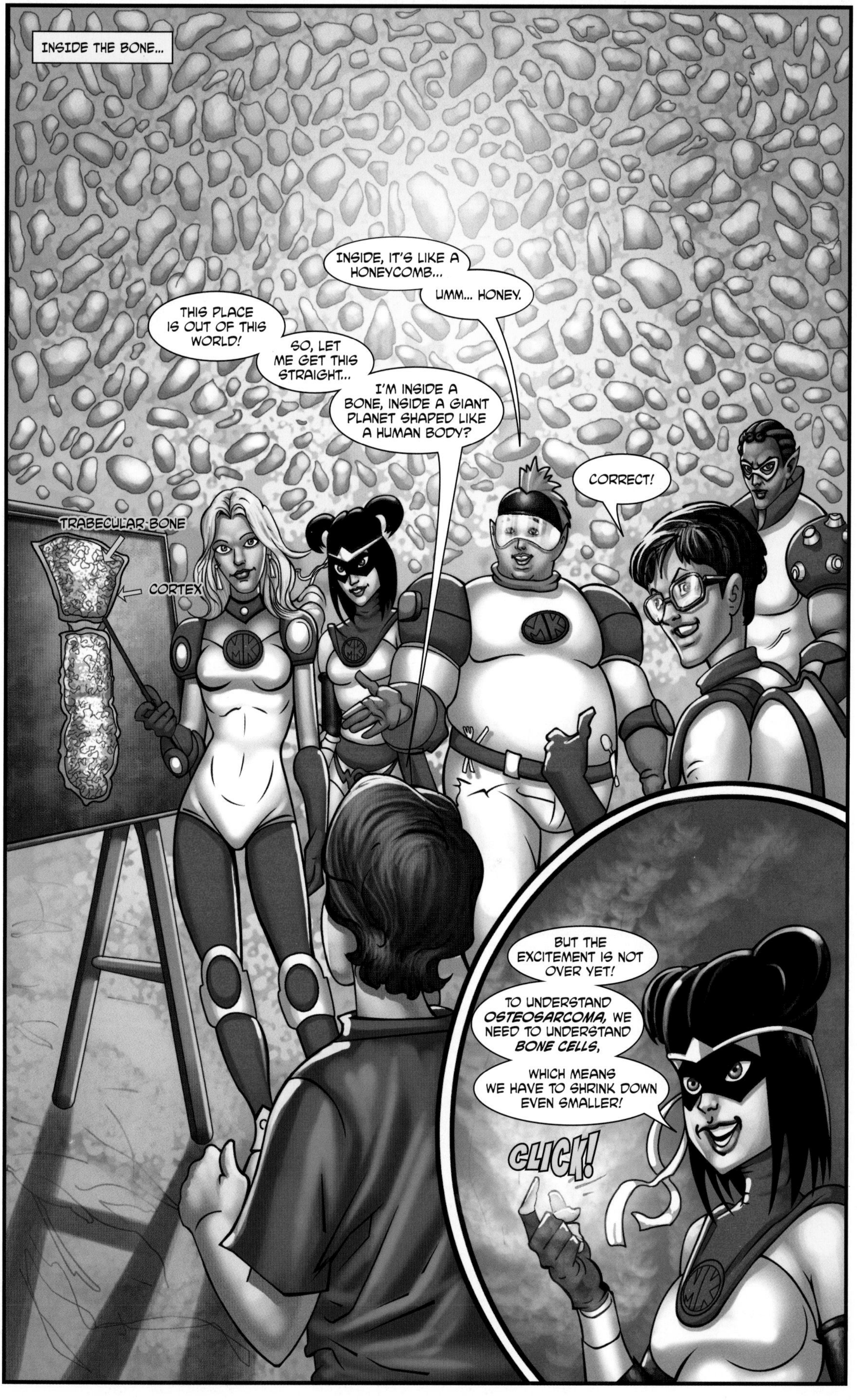
INSIDE THE BONE...
THIS PLACE IS OUT OF THIS WORLD!
INSIDE, IT'S LIKE A HONEYCOMB...
UMM... HONEY.
SO, LET ME GET THIS STRAIGHT...
I'M INSIDE A BONE, INSIDE A GIANT PLANET SHAPED LIKE A HUMAN BODY?
CORRECT!
TRABECULAR BONE
CORTEX
BUT THE EXCITEMENT IS NOT OVER YET!
TO UNDERSTAND *OSTEOSARCOMA*, WE NEED TO UNDERSTAND *BONE CELLS*,
WHICH MEANS WE HAVE TO SHRINK DOWN EVEN SMALLER!
CLICK!

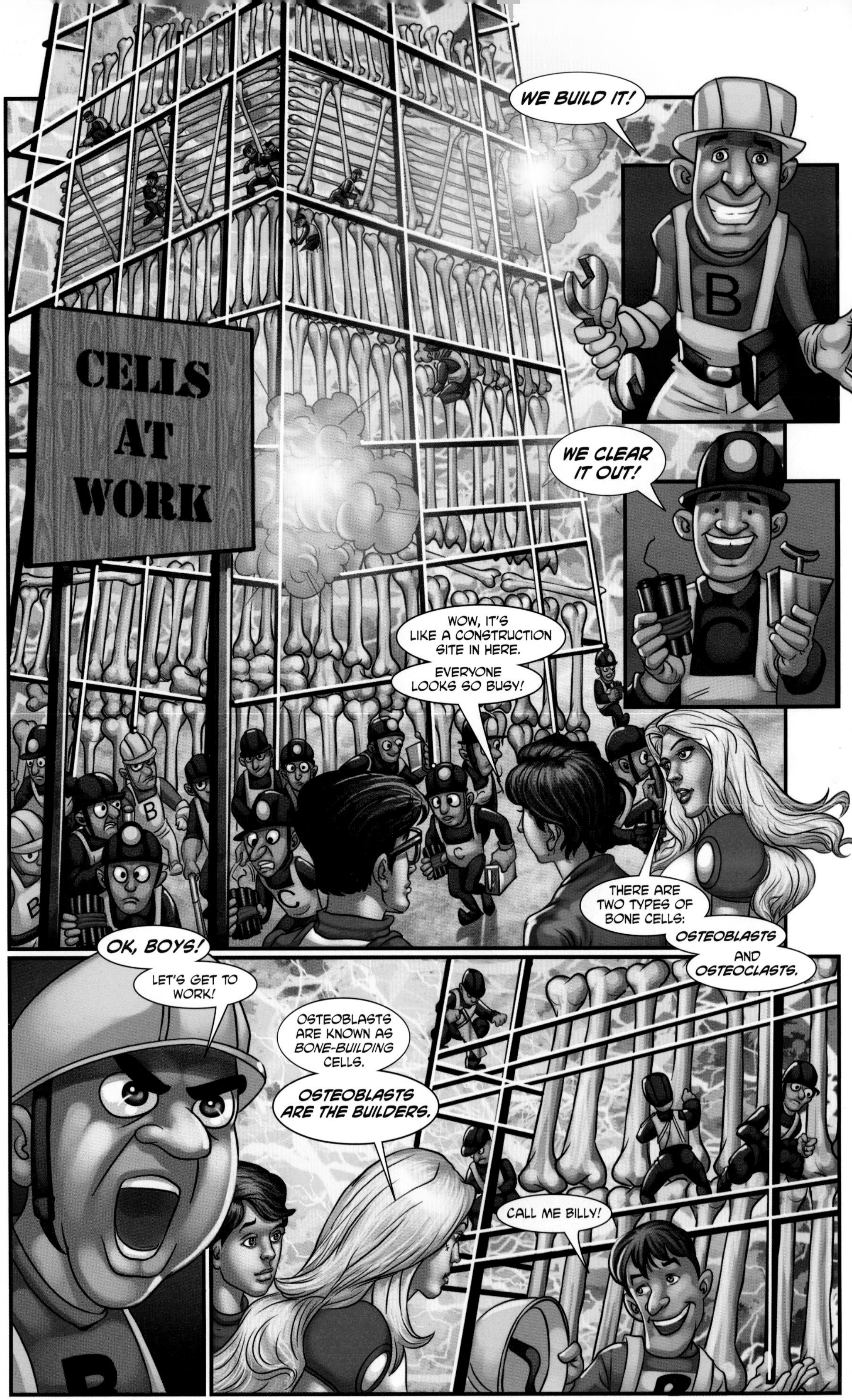
CELLS AT WORK
WE BUILD IT!
WE CLEAR IT OUT!
WOW, IT'S LIKE A CONSTRUCTION SITE IN HERE.
EVERYONE LOOKS SO BUSY!
THERE ARE TWO TYPES OF BONE CELLS:
OSTEOBLASTS AND OSTEOCLASTS.
OK, BOYS!
LET'S GET TO WORK!
OSTEOBLASTS ARE KNOWN AS BONE-BUILDING CELLS.
OSTEOBLASTS ARE THE BUILDERS.
CALL ME BILLY!

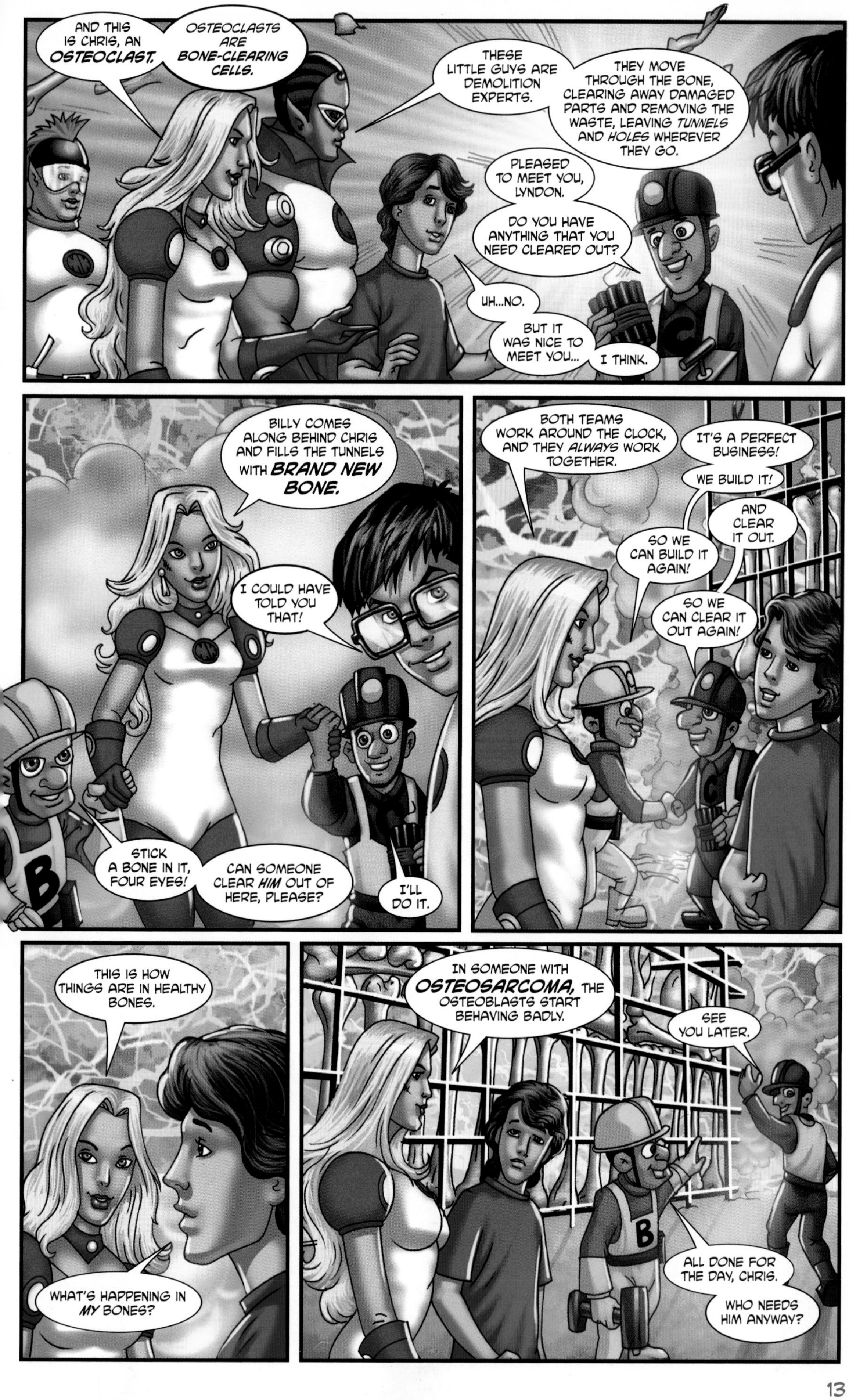
AND THIS IS CHRIS, AN *OSTEOCLAST.*
OSTEOCLASTS ARE BONE-CLEARING CELLS.
THESE LITTLE GUYS ARE DEMOLITION EXPERTS.
THEY MOVE THROUGH THE BONE, CLEARING AWAY DAMAGED PARTS AND REMOVING THE WASTE, LEAVING *TUNNELS* AND *HOLES* WHEREVER THEY GO.
PLEASED TO MEET YOU, LYNDON.
DO YOU HAVE ANYTHING THAT YOU NEED CLEARED OUT?
UH...NO.
BUT IT WAS NICE TO MEET YOU...
I THINK.
BILLY COMES ALONG BEHIND CHRIS AND FILLS THE TUNNELS WITH **BRAND NEW BONE.**
I COULD HAVE TOLD YOU THAT!
STICK A BONE IN IT, FOUR EYES!
CAN SOMEONE CLEAR *HIM* OUT OF HERE, PLEASE?
I'LL DO IT.
BOTH TEAMS WORK AROUND THE CLOCK, AND THEY *ALWAYS* WORK TOGETHER.
IT'S A PERFECT BUSINESS!
WE BUILD IT!
AND CLEAR IT OUT.
SO WE CAN BUILD IT AGAIN!
SO WE CAN CLEAR IT OUT AGAIN!
THIS IS HOW THINGS ARE IN HEALTHY BONES.
WHAT'S HAPPENING IN *MY* BONES?
IN SOMEONE WITH *OSTEOSARCOMA,* THE OSTEOBLASTS START BEHAVING BADLY.
SEE YOU LATER.
ALL DONE FOR THE DAY, CHRIS.
WHO NEEDS HIM ANYWAY?

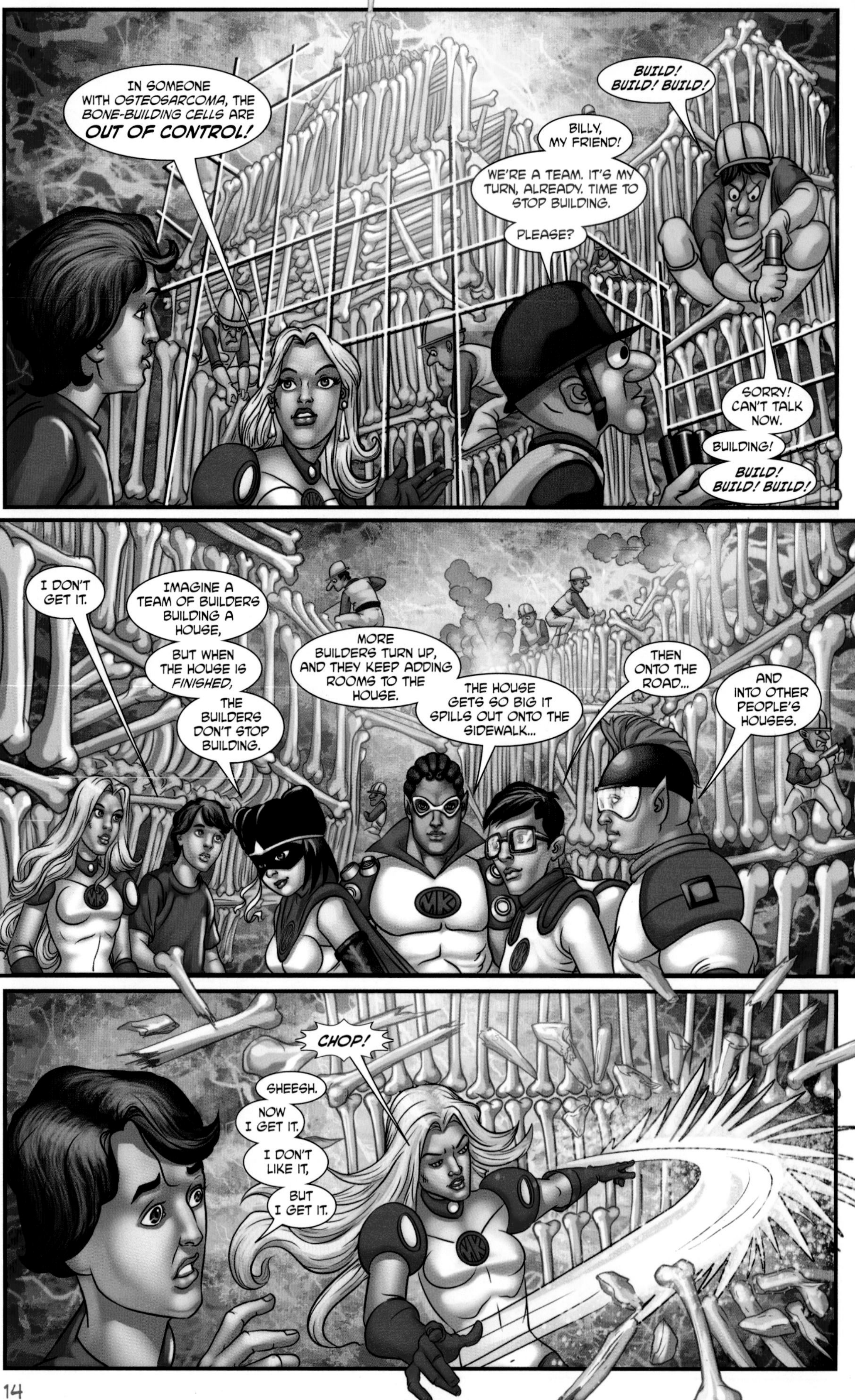
IN SOMEONE WITH OSTEOSARCOMA, THE BONE-BUILDING CELLS ARE OUT OF CONTROL!
BUILD! BUILD! BUILD!
BILLY, MY FRIEND!
WE'RE A TEAM. IT'S MY TURN, ALREADY. TIME TO STOP BUILDING.
PLEASE?
SORRY! CAN'T TALK NOW.
BUILDING!
BUILD! BUILD! BUILD!
I DON'T GET IT.
IMAGINE A TEAM OF BUILDERS BUILDING A HOUSE,
BUT WHEN THE HOUSE IS FINISHED,
THE BUILDERS DON'T STOP BUILDING.
MORE BUILDERS TURN UP, AND THEY KEEP ADDING ROOMS TO THE HOUSE.
THE HOUSE GETS SO BIG IT SPILLS OUT ONTO THE SIDEWALK...
THEN ONTO THE ROAD...
AND INTO OTHER PEOPLE'S HOUSES.
CHOP!
SHEESH.
NOW I GET IT.
I DON'T LIKE IT,
BUT I GET IT.

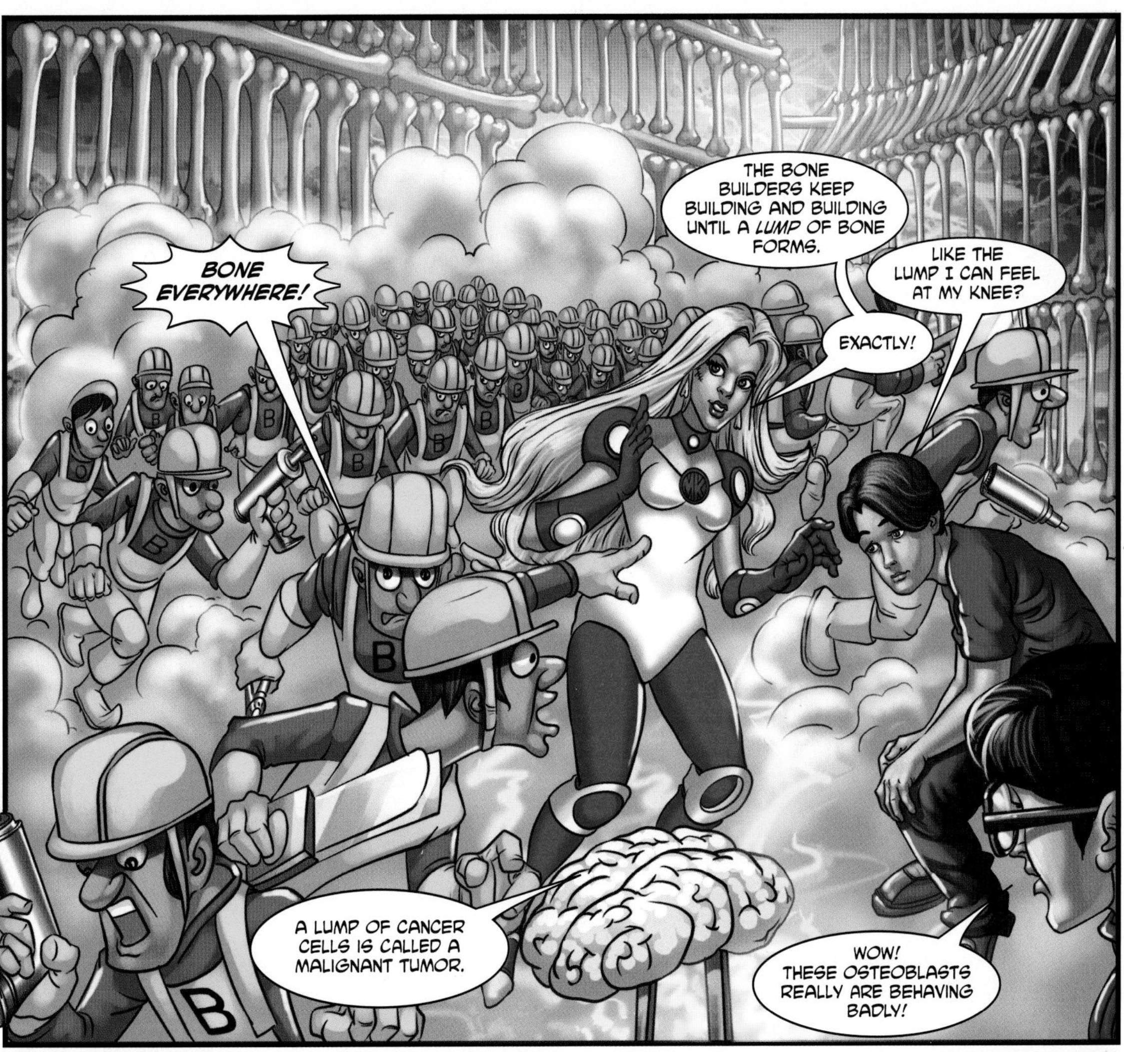
BONE EVERYWHERE!
THE BONE BUILDERS KEEP BUILDING AND BUILDING UNTIL A *LUMP* OF BONE FORMS.
LIKE THE LUMP I CAN FEEL AT MY KNEE?
EXACTLY!
A LUMP OF CANCER CELLS IS CALLED A MALIGNANT TUMOR.
WOW! THESE OSTEOBLASTS REALLY ARE BEHAVING BADLY!

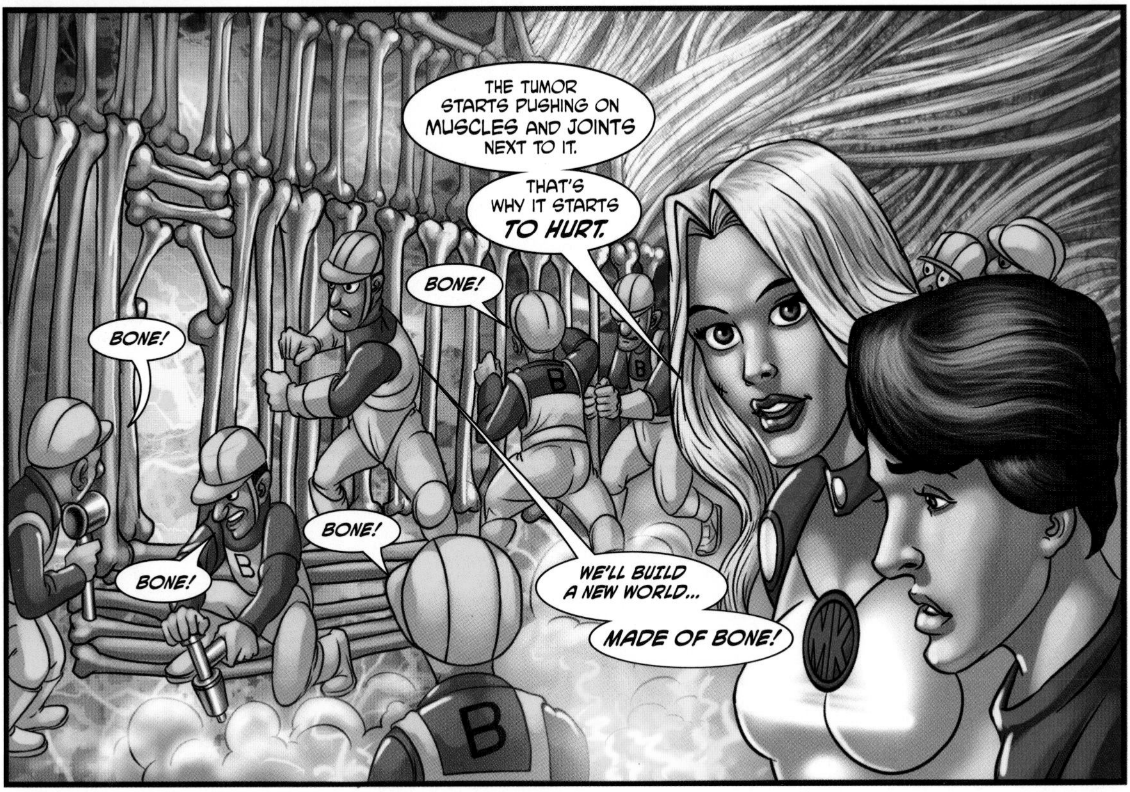
THE TUMOR STARTS PUSHING ON MUSCLES AND JOINTS NEXT TO IT.
THAT'S WHY IT STARTS **TO HURT.**
BONE!
BONE!
BONE!
BONE!
WE'LL BUILD A NEW WORLD...
MADE OF BONE!

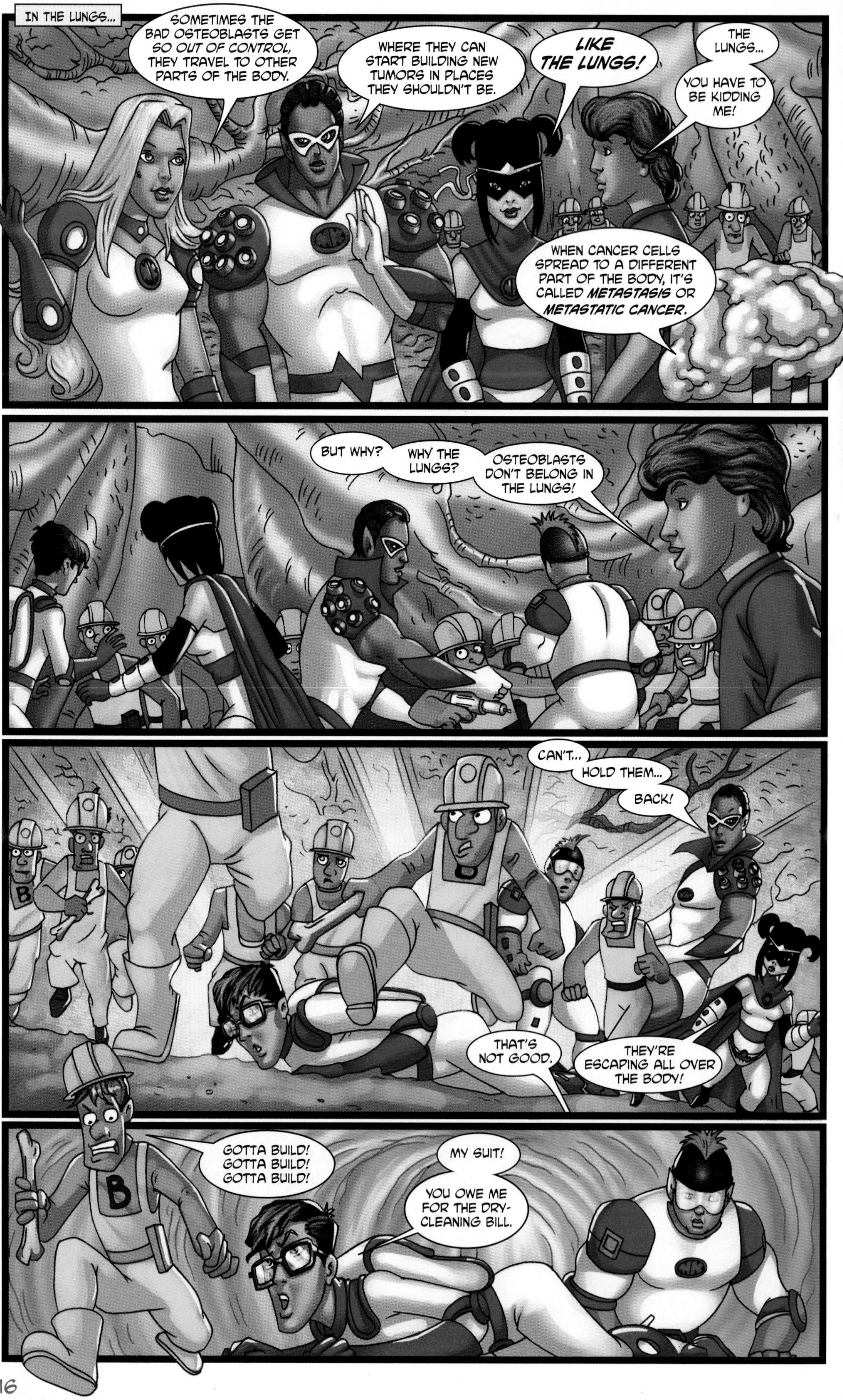
IN THE LUNGS...
SOMETIMES THE BAD OSTEOBLASTS GET SO OUT OF CONTROL, THEY TRAVEL TO OTHER PARTS OF THE BODY.
WHERE THEY CAN START BUILDING NEW TUMORS IN PLACES THEY SHOULDN'T BE.
LIKE THE LUNGS!
THE LUNGS...
YOU HAVE TO BE KIDDING ME!
WHEN CANCER CELLS SPREAD TO A DIFFERENT PART OF THE BODY, IT'S CALLED METASTASIS OR METASTATIC CANCER.
BUT WHY?
WHY THE LUNGS?
OSTEOBLASTS DON'T BELONG IN THE LUNGS!
CAN'T...
HOLD THEM...
BACK!
THAT'S NOT GOOD.
THEY'RE ESCAPING ALL OVER THE BODY!
GOTTA BUILD! GOTTA BUILD! GOTTA BUILD!
MY SUIT!
YOU OWE ME FOR THE DRY-CLEANING BILL.

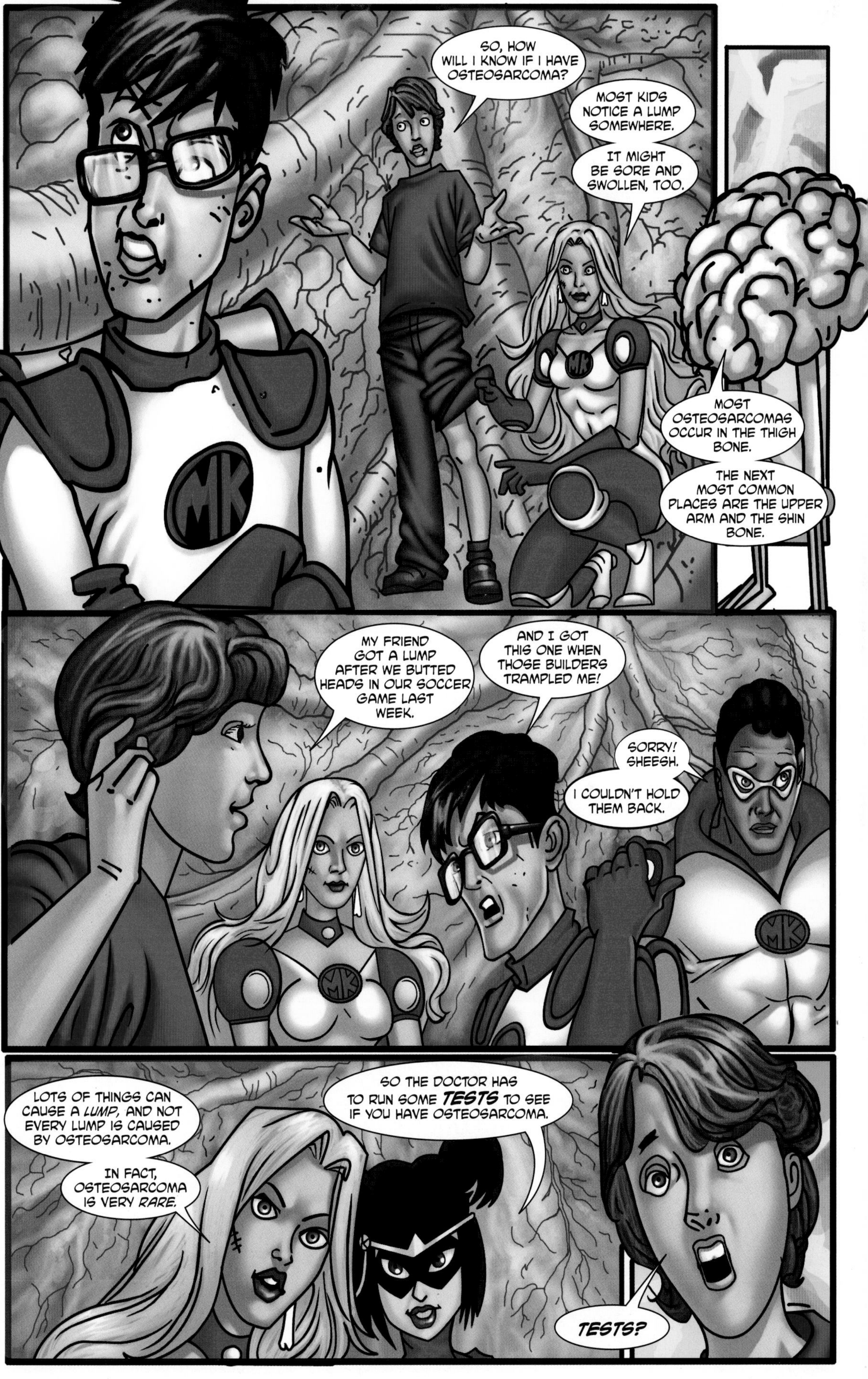
SO, HOW WILL I KNOW IF I HAVE OSTEOSARCOMA?
MOST KIDS NOTICE A LUMP SOMEWHERE.
IT MIGHT BE SORE AND SWOLLEN, TOO.
MOST OSTEOSARCOMAS OCCUR IN THE THIGH BONE.
THE NEXT MOST COMMON PLACES ARE THE UPPER ARM AND THE SHIN BONE.
MY FRIEND GOT A LUMP AFTER WE BUTTED HEADS IN OUR SOCCER GAME LAST WEEK.
AND I GOT THIS ONE WHEN THOSE BUILDERS TRAMPLED ME!
SORRY! SHEESH.
I COULDN'T HOLD THEM BACK.
LOTS OF THINGS CAN CAUSE A *LUMP*, AND NOT EVERY LUMP IS CAUSED BY OSTEOSARCOMA.
IN FACT, OSTEOSARCOMA IS VERY *RARE*.
SO THE DOCTOR HAS TO RUN SOME ***TESTS*** TO SEE IF YOU HAVE OSTEOSARCOMA.
TESTS?

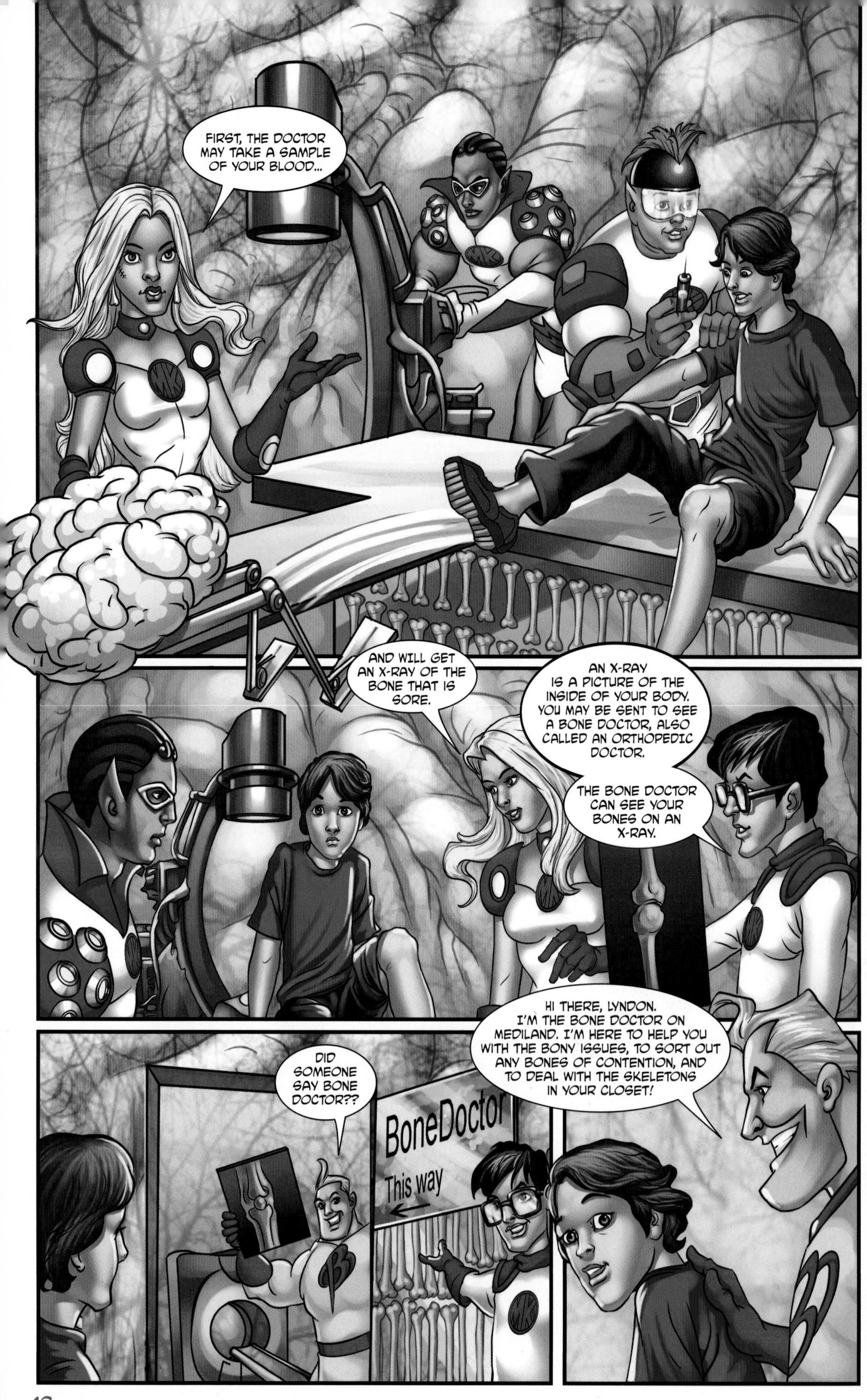
FIRST, THE DOCTOR MAY TAKE A SAMPLE OF YOUR BLOOD...
AND WILL GET AN X-RAY OF THE BONE THAT IS SORE.
AN X-RAY IS A PICTURE OF THE INSIDE OF YOUR BODY. YOU MAY BE SENT TO SEE A BONE DOCTOR, ALSO CALLED AN ORTHOPEDIC DOCTOR.
THE BONE DOCTOR CAN SEE YOUR BONES ON AN X-RAY.
DID SOMEONE SAY BONE DOCTOR??
BoneDoctor
This way
HI THERE, LYNDON. I'M THE BONE DOCTOR ON MEDILAND. I'M HERE TO HELP YOU WITH THE BONY ISSUES, TO SORT OUT ANY BONES OF CONTENTION, AND TO DEAL WITH THE SKELETONS IN YOUR CLOSET!

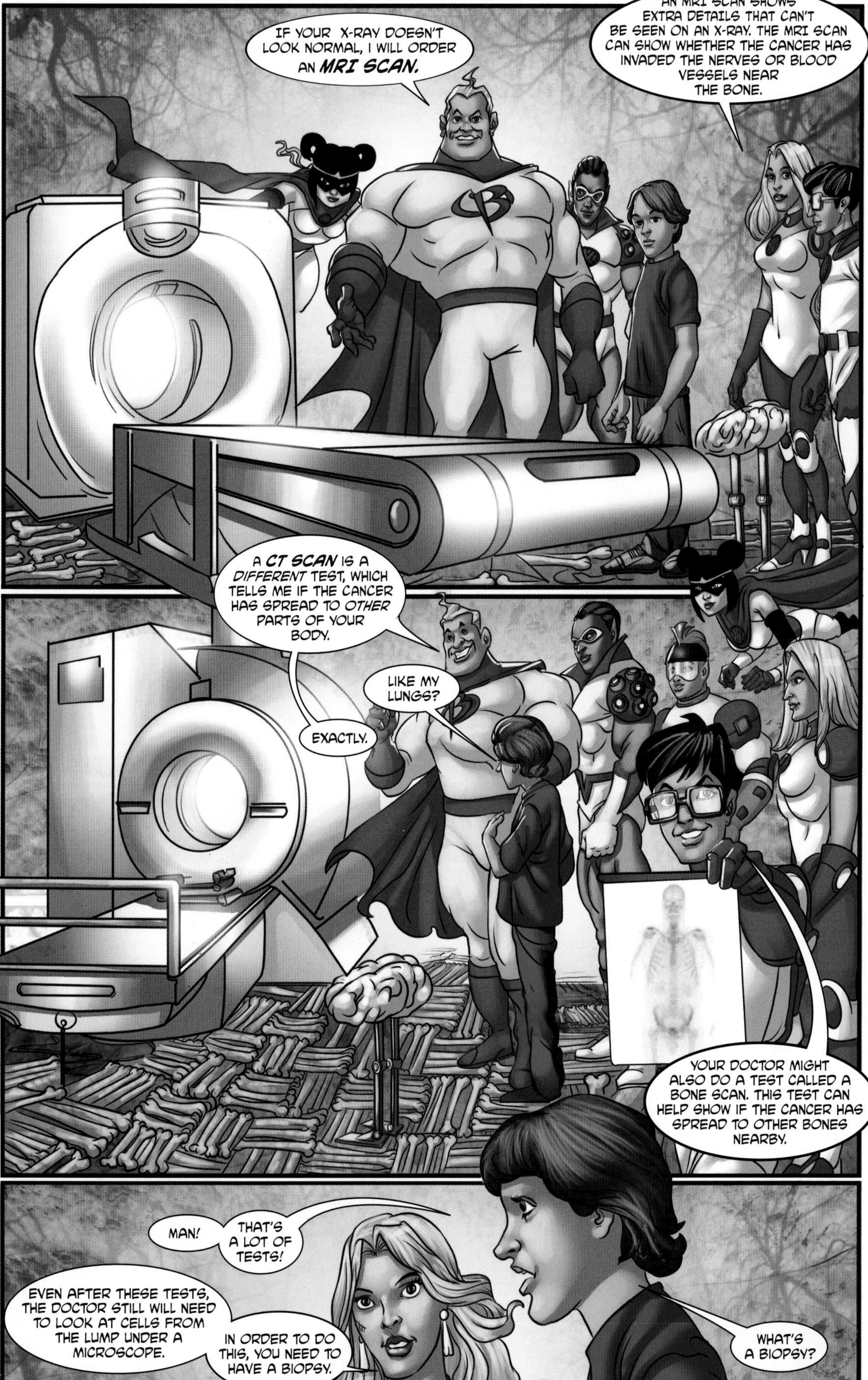
IF YOUR X-RAY DOESN'T LOOK NORMAL, I WILL ORDER AN MRI SCAN.
AN MRI SCAN SHOWS EXTRA DETAILS THAT CAN'T BE SEEN ON AN X-RAY. THE MRI SCAN CAN SHOW WHETHER THE CANCER HAS INVADED THE NERVES OR BLOOD VESSELS NEAR THE BONE.
A CT SCAN IS A DIFFERENT TEST, WHICH TELLS ME IF THE CANCER HAS SPREAD TO OTHER PARTS OF YOUR BODY.
LIKE MY LUNGS?
EXACTLY.
YOUR DOCTOR MIGHT ALSO DO A TEST CALLED A BONE SCAN. THIS TEST CAN HELP SHOW IF THE CANCER HAS SPREAD TO OTHER BONES NEARBY.
MAN!
THAT'S A LOT OF TESTS!
EVEN AFTER THESE TESTS, THE DOCTOR STILL WILL NEED TO LOOK AT CELLS FROM THE LUMP UNDER A MICROSCOPE.
IN ORDER TO DO THIS, YOU NEED TO HAVE A BIOPSY.
WHAT'S A BIOPSY?

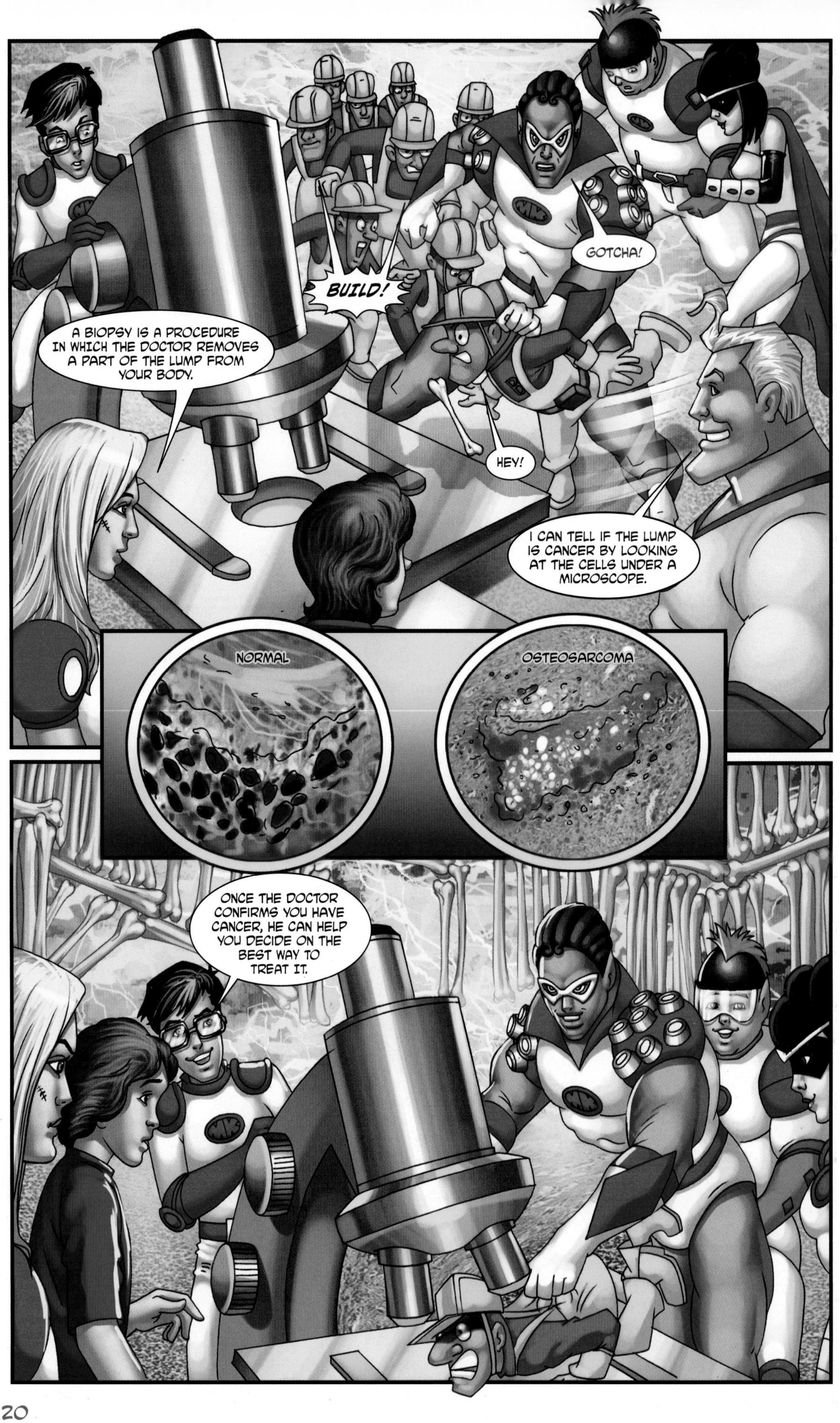
BUILD!
GOTCHA!
A BIOPSY IS A PROCEDURE IN WHICH THE DOCTOR REMOVES A PART OF THE LUMP FROM YOUR BODY.
HEY!
I CAN TELL IF THE LUMP IS CANCER BY LOOKING AT THE CELLS UNDER A MICROSCOPE.
NORMAL
OSTEOSARCOMA
ONCE THE DOCTOR CONFIRMS YOU HAVE CANCER, HE CAN HELP YOU DECIDE ON THE BEST WAY TO TREAT IT.

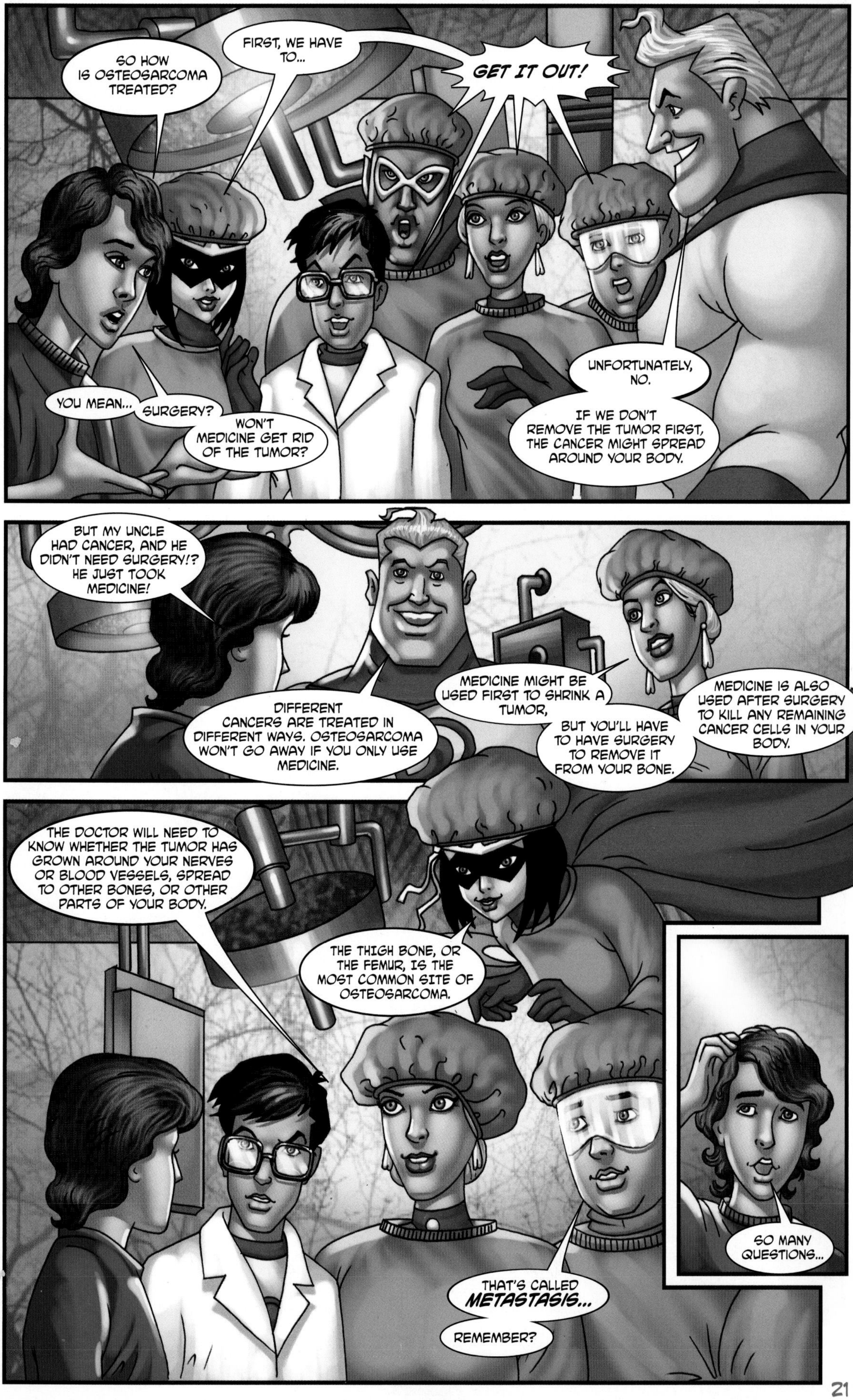
SO HOW IS OSTEOSARCOMA TREATED?
FIRST, WE HAVE TO...
GET IT OUT!
YOU MEAN...
SURGERY?
WON'T MEDICINE GET RID OF THE TUMOR?
UNFORTUNATELY, NO.
IF WE DON'T REMOVE THE TUMOR FIRST, THE CANCER MIGHT SPREAD AROUND YOUR BODY.
BUT MY UNCLE HAD CANCER, AND HE DIDN'T NEED SURGERY!? HE JUST TOOK MEDICINE!
DIFFERENT CANCERS ARE TREATED IN DIFFERENT WAYS. OSTEOSARCOMA WON'T GO AWAY IF YOU ONLY USE MEDICINE.
MEDICINE MIGHT BE USED FIRST TO SHRINK A TUMOR,
BUT YOU'LL HAVE TO HAVE SURGERY TO REMOVE IT FROM YOUR BONE.
MEDICINE IS ALSO USED AFTER SURGERY TO KILL ANY REMAINING CANCER CELLS IN YOUR BODY.
THE DOCTOR WILL NEED TO KNOW WHETHER THE TUMOR HAS GROWN AROUND YOUR NERVES OR BLOOD VESSELS, SPREAD TO OTHER BONES, OR OTHER PARTS OF YOUR BODY.
THE THIGH BONE, OR THE FEMUR, IS THE MOST COMMON SITE OF OSTEOSARCOMA.
THAT'S CALLED METASTASIS...
REMEMBER?
SO MANY QUESTIONS...

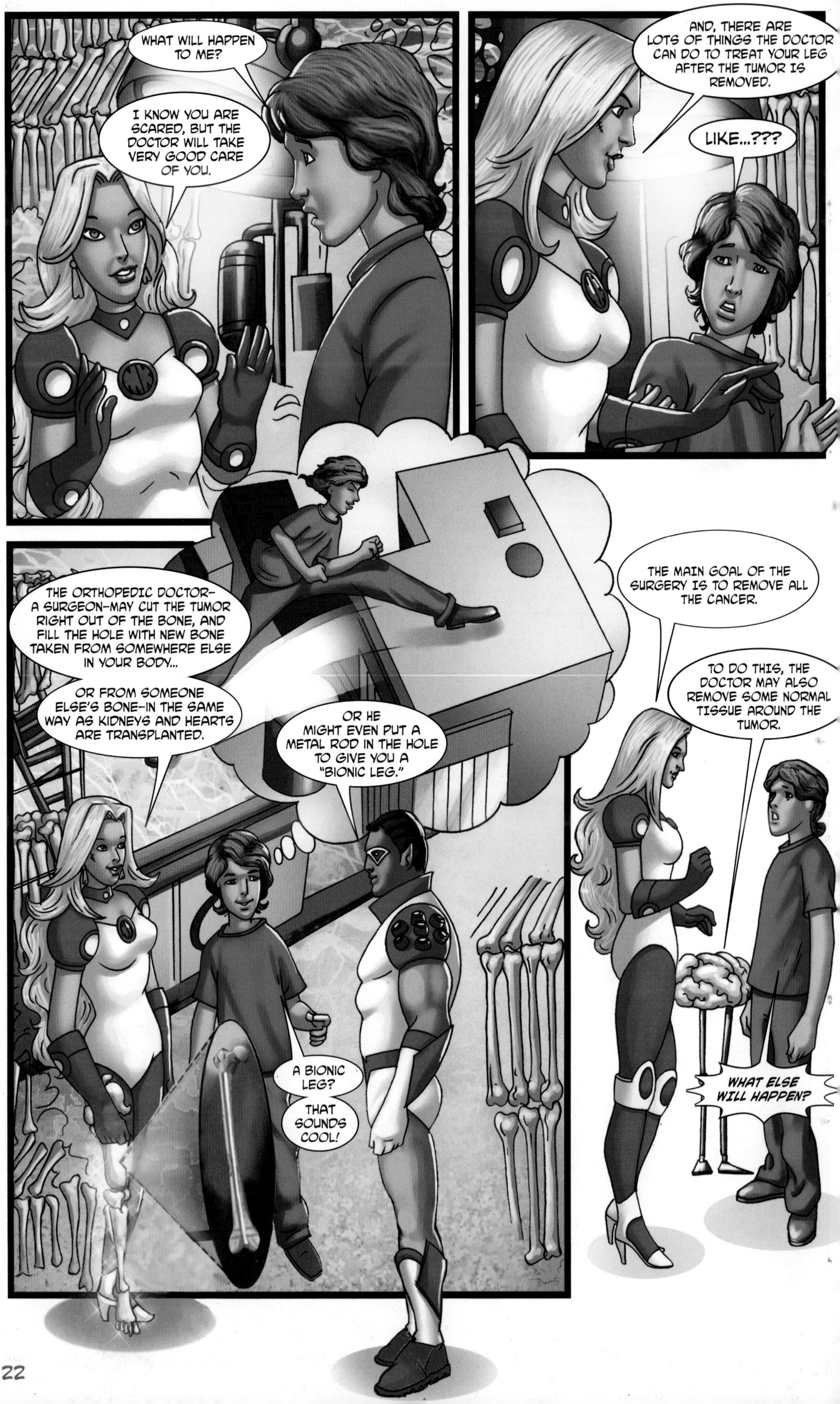
WHAT WILL HAPPEN TO ME?
I KNOW YOU ARE SCARED, BUT THE DOCTOR WILL TAKE VERY GOOD CARE OF YOU.
AND, THERE ARE LOTS OF THINGS THE DOCTOR CAN DO TO TREAT YOUR LEG AFTER THE TUMOR IS REMOVED.
LIKE...???
THE ORTHOPEDIC DOCTOR–A SURGEON–MAY CUT THE TUMOR RIGHT OUT OF THE BONE, AND FILL THE HOLE WITH NEW BONE TAKEN FROM SOMEWHERE ELSE IN YOUR BODY...
OR FROM SOMEONE ELSE'S BONE–IN THE SAME WAY AS KIDNEYS AND HEARTS ARE TRANSPLANTED.
OR HE MIGHT EVEN PUT A METAL ROD IN THE HOLE TO GIVE YOU A "BIONIC LEG."
A BIONIC LEG?
THAT SOUNDS COOL!
THE MAIN GOAL OF THE SURGERY IS TO REMOVE ALL THE CANCER.
TO DO THIS, THE DOCTOR MAY ALSO REMOVE SOME NORMAL TISSUE AROUND THE TUMOR.
WHAT ELSE WILL HAPPEN?

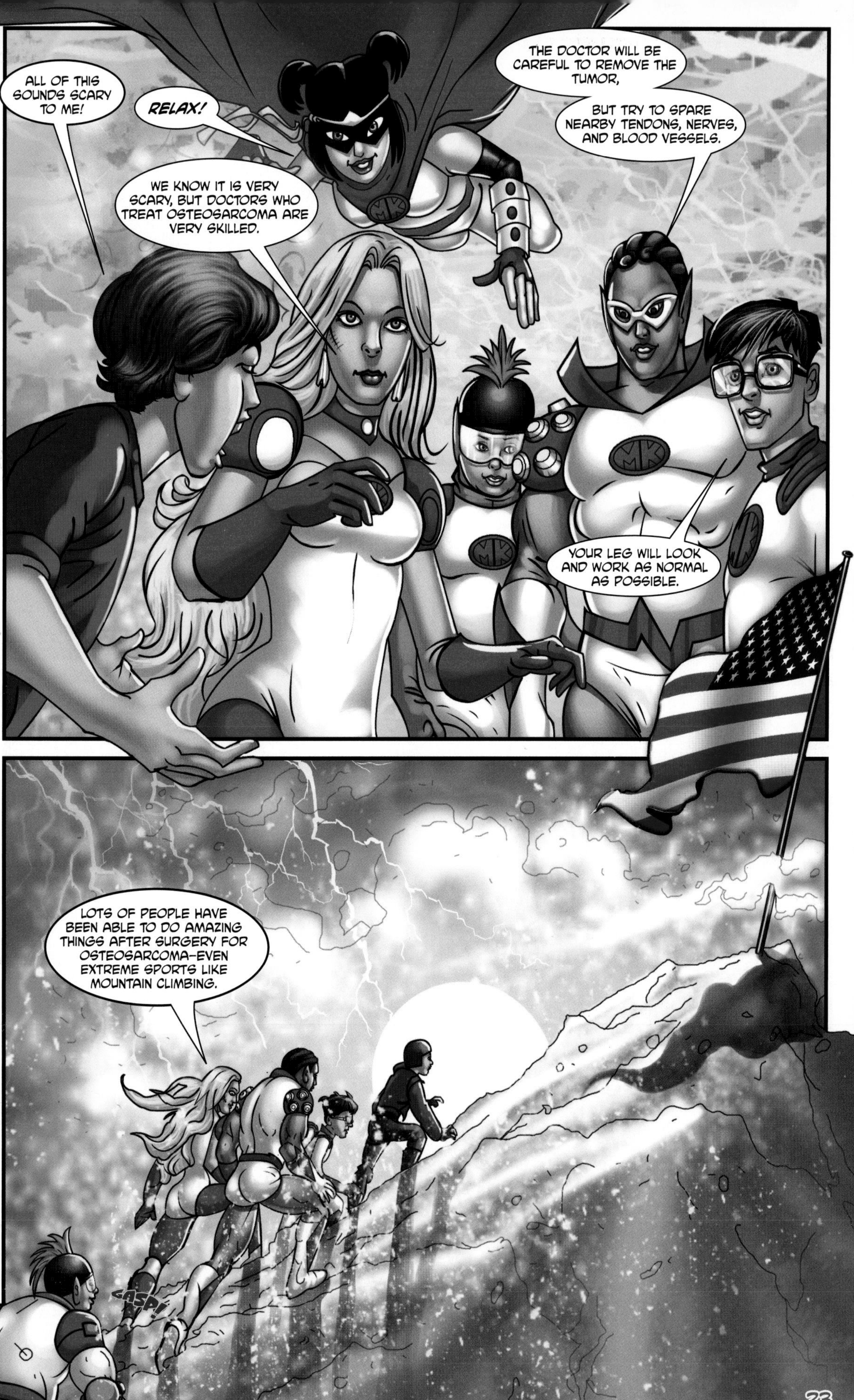
ALL OF THIS SOUNDS SCARY TO ME!
RELAX!
THE DOCTOR WILL BE CAREFUL TO REMOVE THE TUMOR,
BUT TRY TO SPARE NEARBY TENDONS, NERVES, AND BLOOD VESSELS.
WE KNOW IT IS VERY SCARY, BUT DOCTORS WHO TREAT OSTEOSARCOMA ARE VERY SKILLED.
YOUR LEG WILL LOOK AND WORK AS NORMAL AS POSSIBLE.
LOTS OF PEOPLE HAVE BEEN ABLE TO DO AMAZING THINGS AFTER SURGERY FOR OSTEOSARCOMA–EVEN EXTREME SPORTS LIKE MOUNTAIN CLIMBING.
GASP!

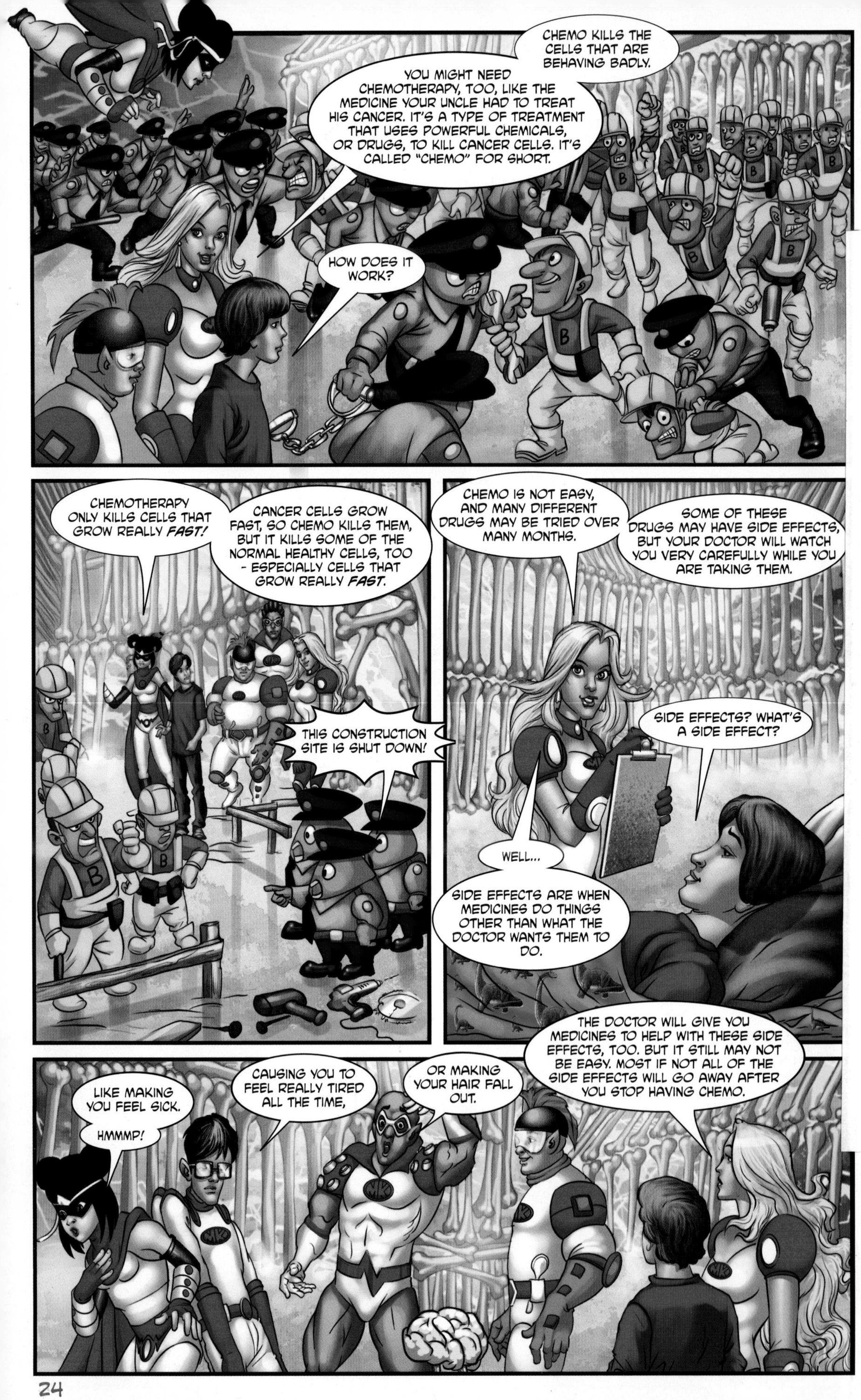
YOU MIGHT NEED CHEMOTHERAPY, TOO, LIKE THE MEDICINE YOUR UNCLE HAD TO TREAT HIS CANCER. IT'S A TYPE OF TREATMENT THAT USES POWERFUL CHEMICALS, OR DRUGS, TO KILL CANCER CELLS. IT'S CALLED "CHEMO" FOR SHORT.
CHEMO KILLS THE CELLS THAT ARE BEHAVING BADLY.
HOW DOES IT WORK?
CHEMOTHERAPY ONLY KILLS CELLS THAT GROW REALLY *FAST!*
CANCER CELLS GROW FAST, SO CHEMO KILLS THEM, BUT IT KILLS SOME OF THE NORMAL HEALTHY CELLS, TOO - ESPECIALLY CELLS THAT GROW REALLY *FAST*.
THIS CONSTRUCTION SITE IS SHUT DOWN!
CHEMO IS NOT EASY, AND MANY DIFFERENT DRUGS MAY BE TRIED OVER MANY MONTHS.
SOME OF THESE DRUGS MAY HAVE SIDE EFFECTS, BUT YOUR DOCTOR WILL WATCH YOU VERY CAREFULLY WHILE YOU ARE TAKING THEM.
SIDE EFFECTS? WHAT'S A SIDE EFFECT?
WELL...
SIDE EFFECTS ARE WHEN MEDICINES DO THINGS OTHER THAN WHAT THE DOCTOR WANTS THEM TO DO.
LIKE MAKING YOU FEEL SICK.
HMMMP!
CAUSING YOU TO FEEL REALLY TIRED ALL THE TIME,
OR MAKING YOUR HAIR FALL OUT.
THE DOCTOR WILL GIVE YOU MEDICINES TO HELP WITH THESE SIDE EFFECTS, TOO. BUT IT STILL MAY NOT BE EASY. MOST IF NOT ALL OF THE SIDE EFFECTS WILL GO AWAY AFTER YOU STOP HAVING CHEMO.

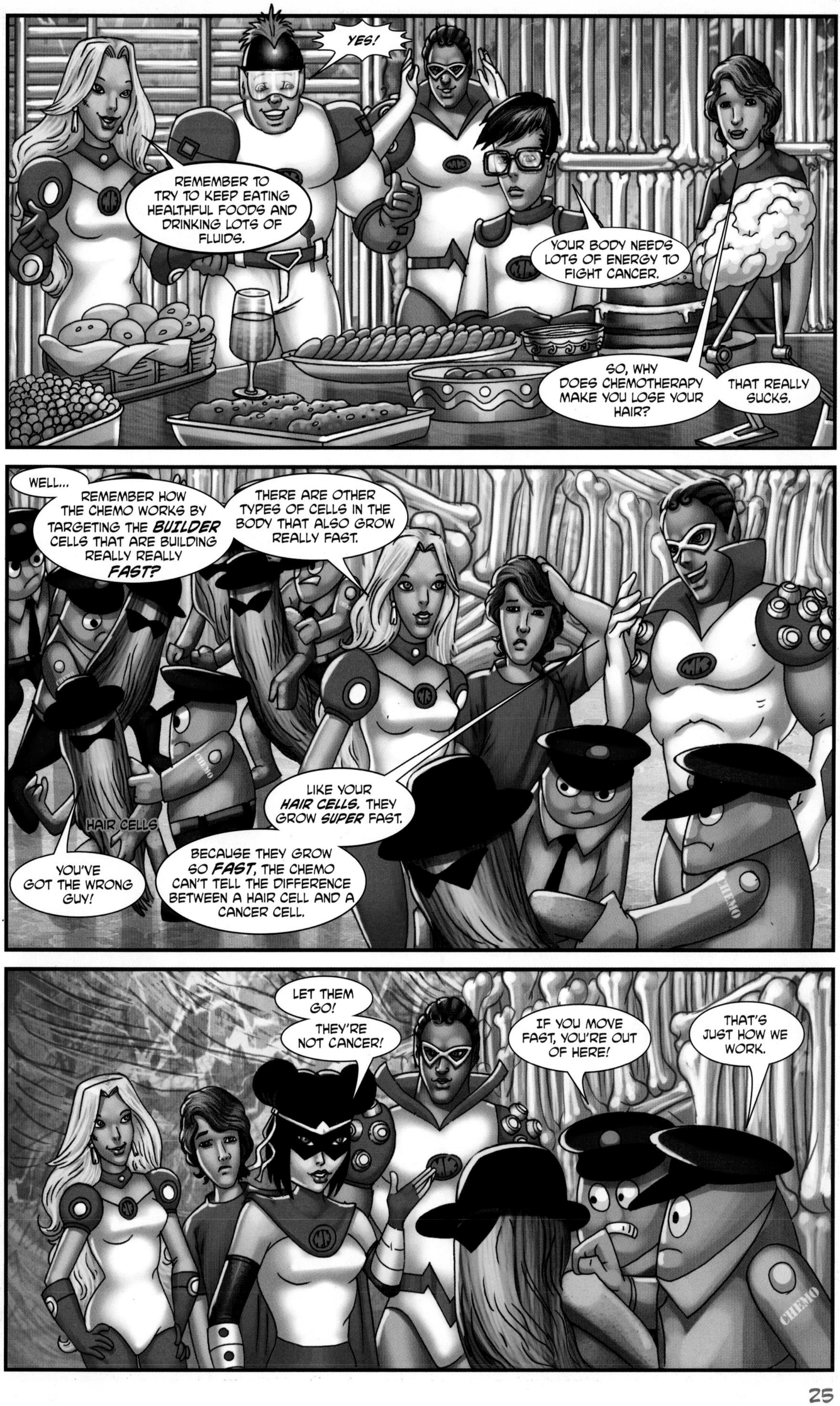
REMEMBER TO TRY TO KEEP EATING HEALTHFUL FOODS AND DRINKING LOTS OF FLUIDS.
YES!
YOUR BODY NEEDS LOTS OF ENERGY TO FIGHT CANCER.
SO, WHY DOES CHEMOTHERAPY MAKE YOU LOSE YOUR HAIR?
THAT REALLY SUCKS.
WELL...
REMEMBER HOW THE CHEMO WORKS BY TARGETING THE **BUILDER** CELLS THAT ARE BUILDING REALLY REALLY ***FAST?***
THERE ARE OTHER TYPES OF CELLS IN THE BODY THAT ALSO GROW REALLY FAST.
LIKE YOUR ***HAIR CELLS.*** THEY GROW ***SUPER*** FAST.
HAIR CELLS
YOU'VE GOT THE WRONG GUY!
BECAUSE THEY GROW SO ***FAST***, THE CHEMO CAN'T TELL THE DIFFERENCE BETWEEN A HAIR CELL AND A CANCER CELL.
CHEMO
LET THEM GO!
THEY'RE NOT CANCER!
IF YOU MOVE FAST, YOU'RE OUT OF HERE!
THAT'S JUST HOW WE WORK.
CHEMO

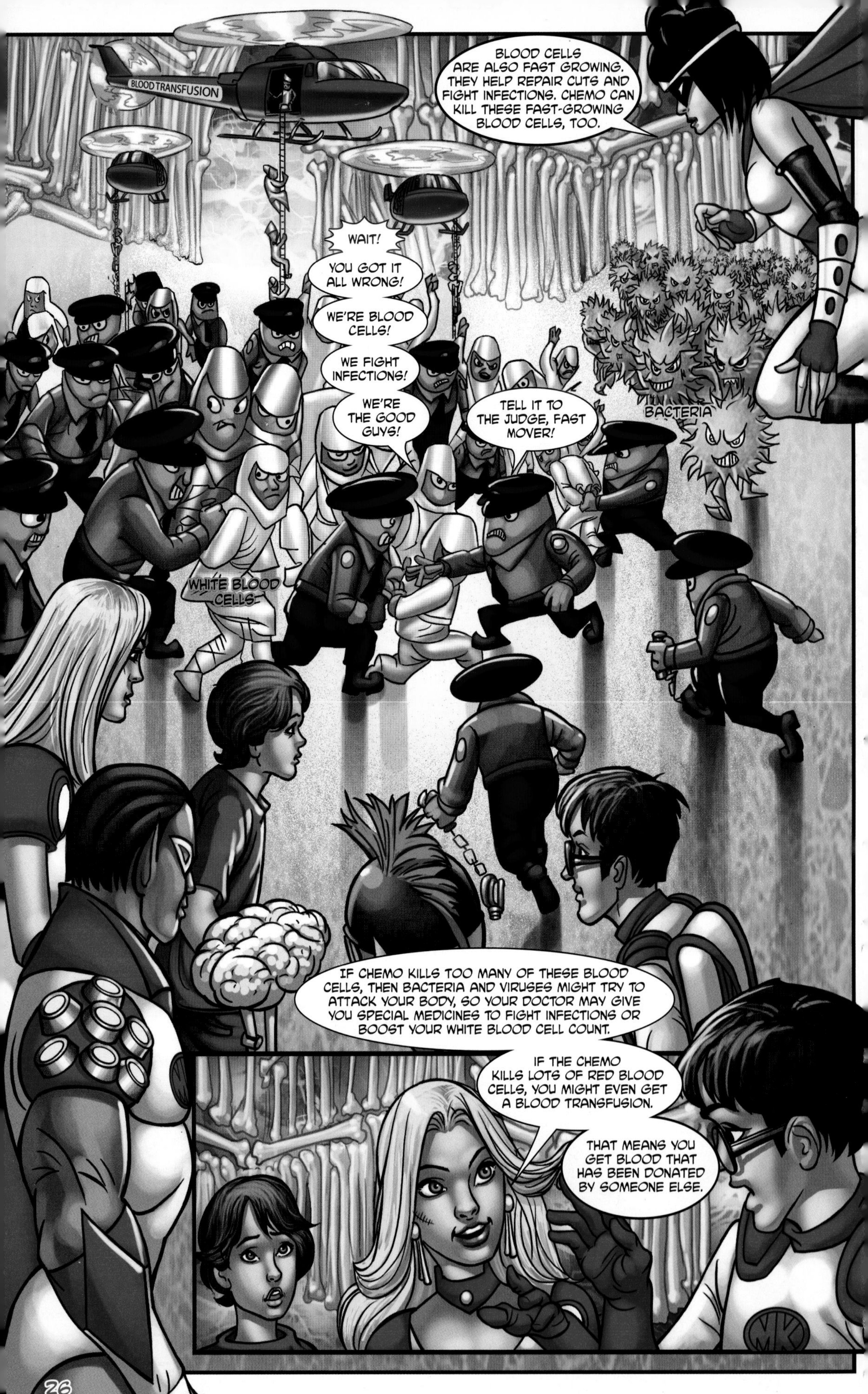
BLOOD TRANSFUSION
BLOOD CELLS ARE ALSO FAST GROWING. THEY HELP REPAIR CUTS AND FIGHT INFECTIONS. CHEMO CAN KILL THESE FAST-GROWING BLOOD CELLS, TOO.
WAIT!
YOU GOT IT ALL WRONG!
WE'RE BLOOD CELLS!
WE FIGHT INFECTIONS!
WE'RE THE GOOD GUYS!
TELL IT TO THE JUDGE, FAST MOVER!
BACTERIA
WHITE BLOOD CELLS
IF CHEMO KILLS TOO MANY OF THESE BLOOD CELLS, THEN BACTERIA AND VIRUSES MIGHT TRY TO ATTACK YOUR BODY, SO YOUR DOCTOR MAY GIVE YOU SPECIAL MEDICINES TO FIGHT INFECTIONS OR BOOST YOUR WHITE BLOOD CELL COUNT.
IF THE CHEMO KILLS LOTS OF RED BLOOD CELLS, YOU MIGHT EVEN GET A BLOOD TRANSFUSION.
THAT MEANS YOU GET BLOOD THAT HAS BEEN DONATED BY SOMEONE ELSE.
MK

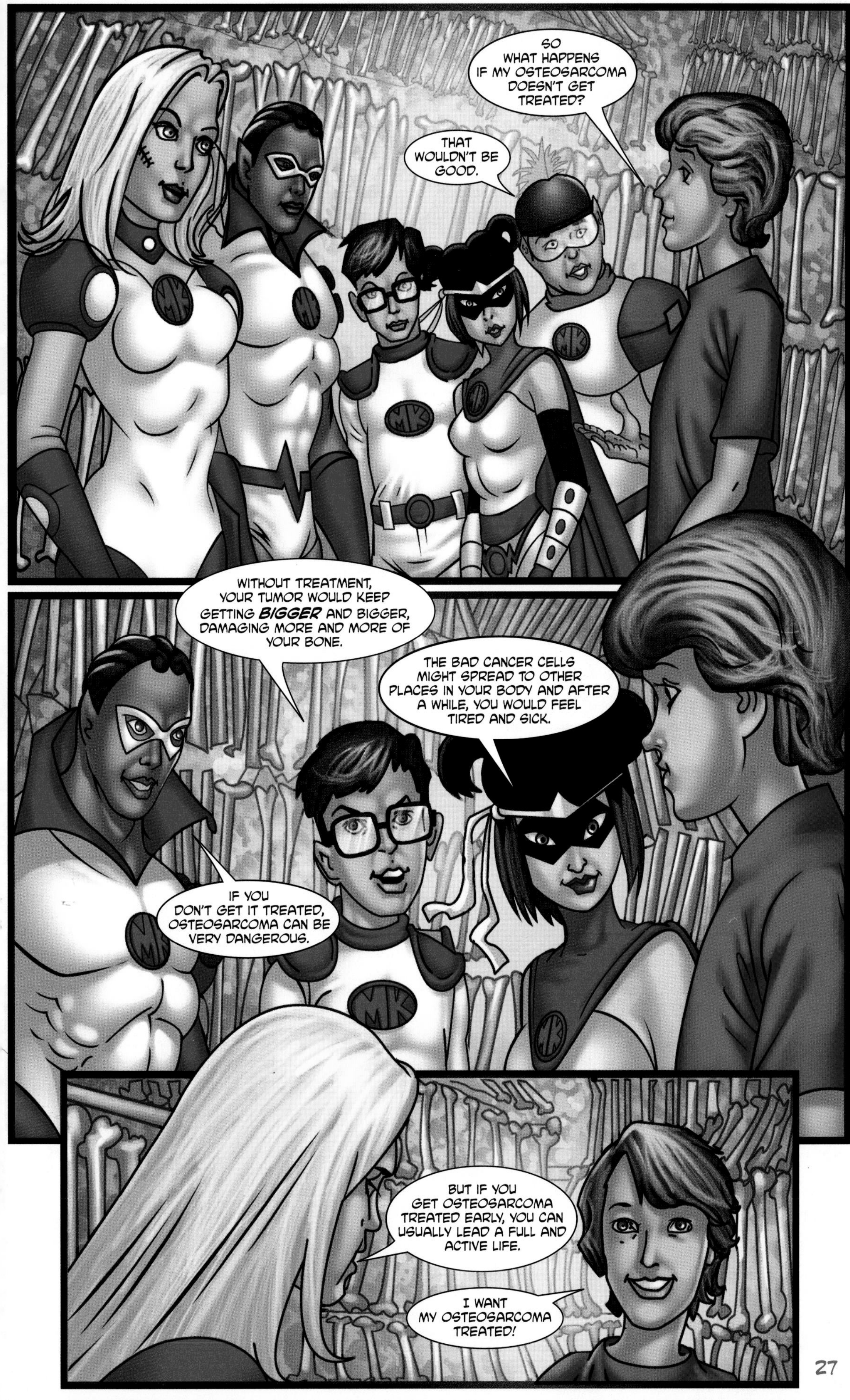
SO WHAT HAPPENS IF MY OSTEOSARCOMA DOESN'T GET TREATED?
THAT WOULDN'T BE GOOD.
WITHOUT TREATMENT, YOUR TUMOR WOULD KEEP GETTING ***BIGGER*** AND BIGGER, DAMAGING MORE AND MORE OF YOUR BONE.
THE BAD CANCER CELLS MIGHT SPREAD TO OTHER PLACES IN YOUR BODY AND AFTER A WHILE, YOU WOULD FEEL TIRED AND SICK.
IF YOU DON'T GET IT TREATED, OSTEOSARCOMA CAN BE VERY DANGEROUS.
BUT IF YOU GET OSTEOSARCOMA TREATED EARLY, YOU CAN USUALLY LEAD A FULL AND ACTIVE LIFE.
I WANT MY OSTEOSARCOMA TREATED!

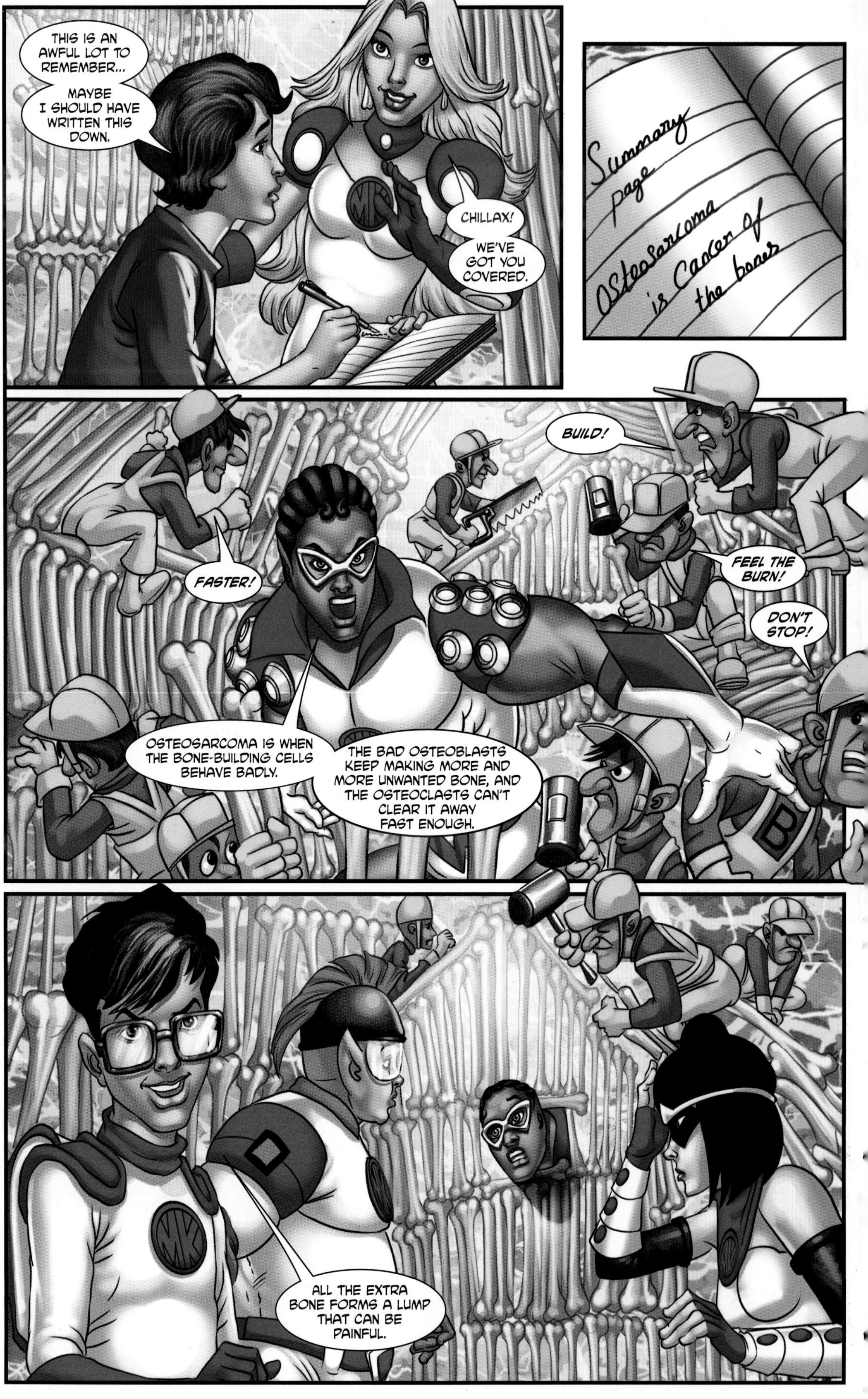
THIS IS AN AWFUL LOT TO REMEMBER...
MAYBE I SHOULD HAVE WRITTEN THIS DOWN.
CHILLAX!
WE'VE GOT YOU COVERED.
Summary page
Osteosarcoma is Cancer of the bones
BUILD!
FASTER!
FEEL THE BURN!
DON'T STOP!
OSTEOSARCOMA IS WHEN THE BONE-BUILDING CELLS BEHAVE BADLY.
THE BAD OSTEOBLASTS KEEP MAKING MORE AND MORE UNWANTED BONE, AND THE OSTEOCLASTS CAN'T CLEAR IT AWAY FAST ENOUGH.
B
ALL THE EXTRA BONE FORMS A LUMP THAT CAN BE PAINFUL.

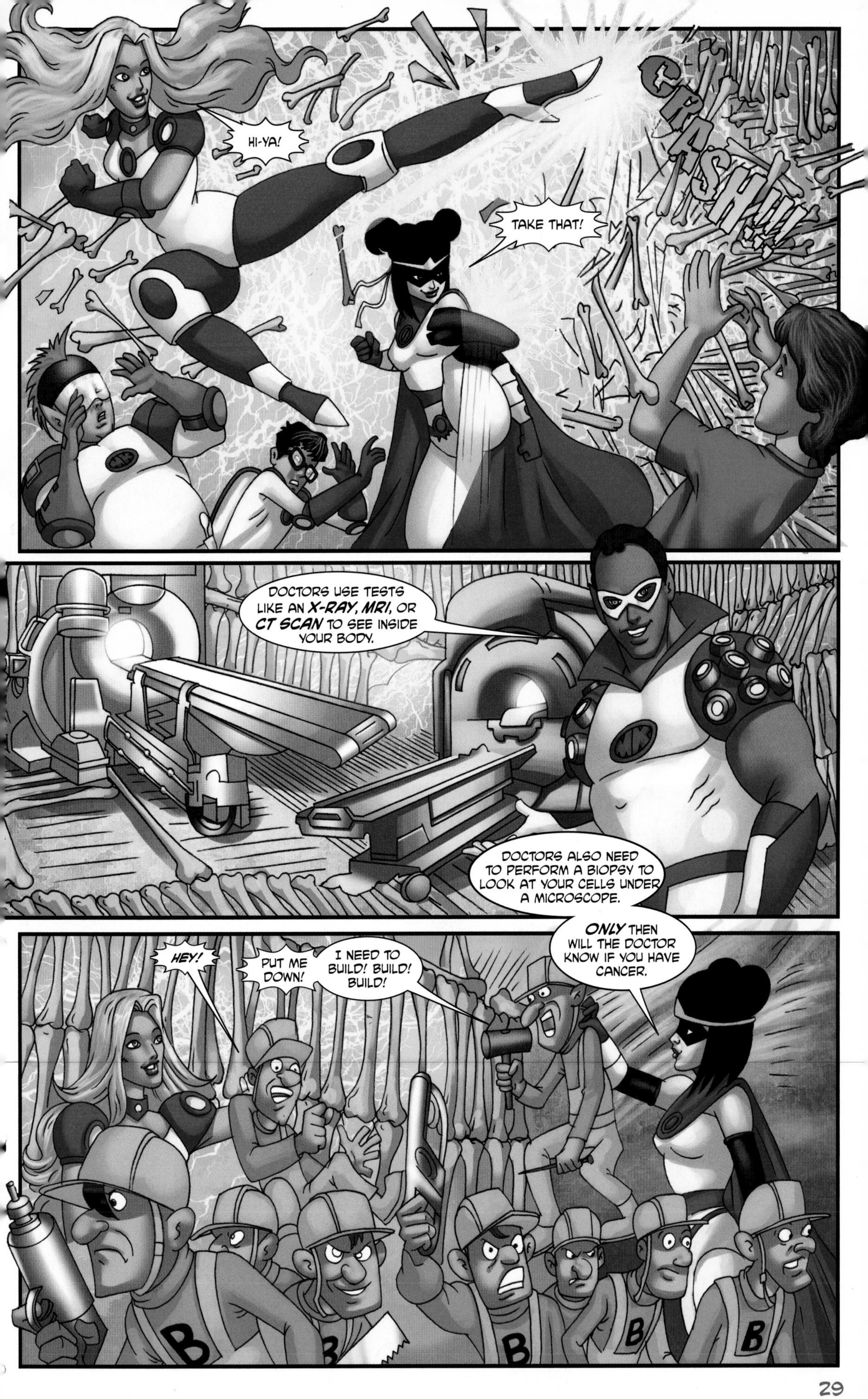
HI-YA!
CRASH!!!
TAKE THAT!
DOCTORS USE TESTS LIKE AN X-RAY, MRI, OR CT SCAN TO SEE INSIDE YOUR BODY.
DOCTORS ALSO NEED TO PERFORM A BIOPSY TO LOOK AT YOUR CELLS UNDER A MICROSCOPE.
HEY!
PUT ME DOWN!
I NEED TO BUILD! BUILD! BUILD!
ONLY THEN WILL THE DOCTOR KNOW IF YOU HAVE CANCER.
B
B
B
B
B

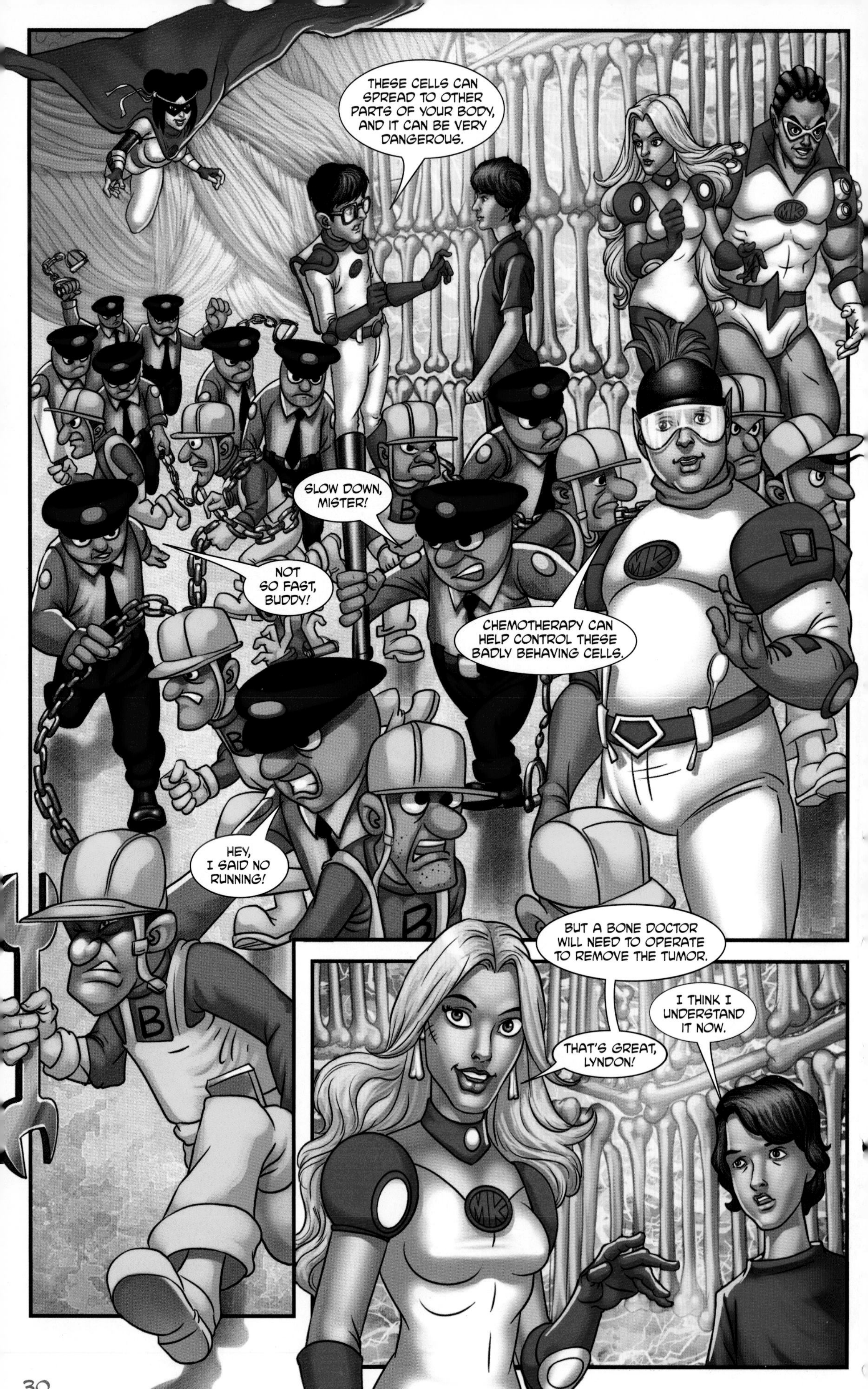
THESE CELLS CAN SPREAD TO OTHER PARTS OF YOUR BODY, AND IT CAN BE VERY DANGEROUS.
SLOW DOWN, MISTER!
NOT SO FAST, BUDDY!
CHEMOTHERAPY CAN HELP CONTROL THESE BADLY BEHAVING CELLS.
HEY, I SAID NO RUNNING!
BUT A BONE DOCTOR WILL NEED TO OPERATE TO REMOVE THE TUMOR.
I THINK I UNDERSTAND IT NOW.
THAT'S GREAT, LYNDON!

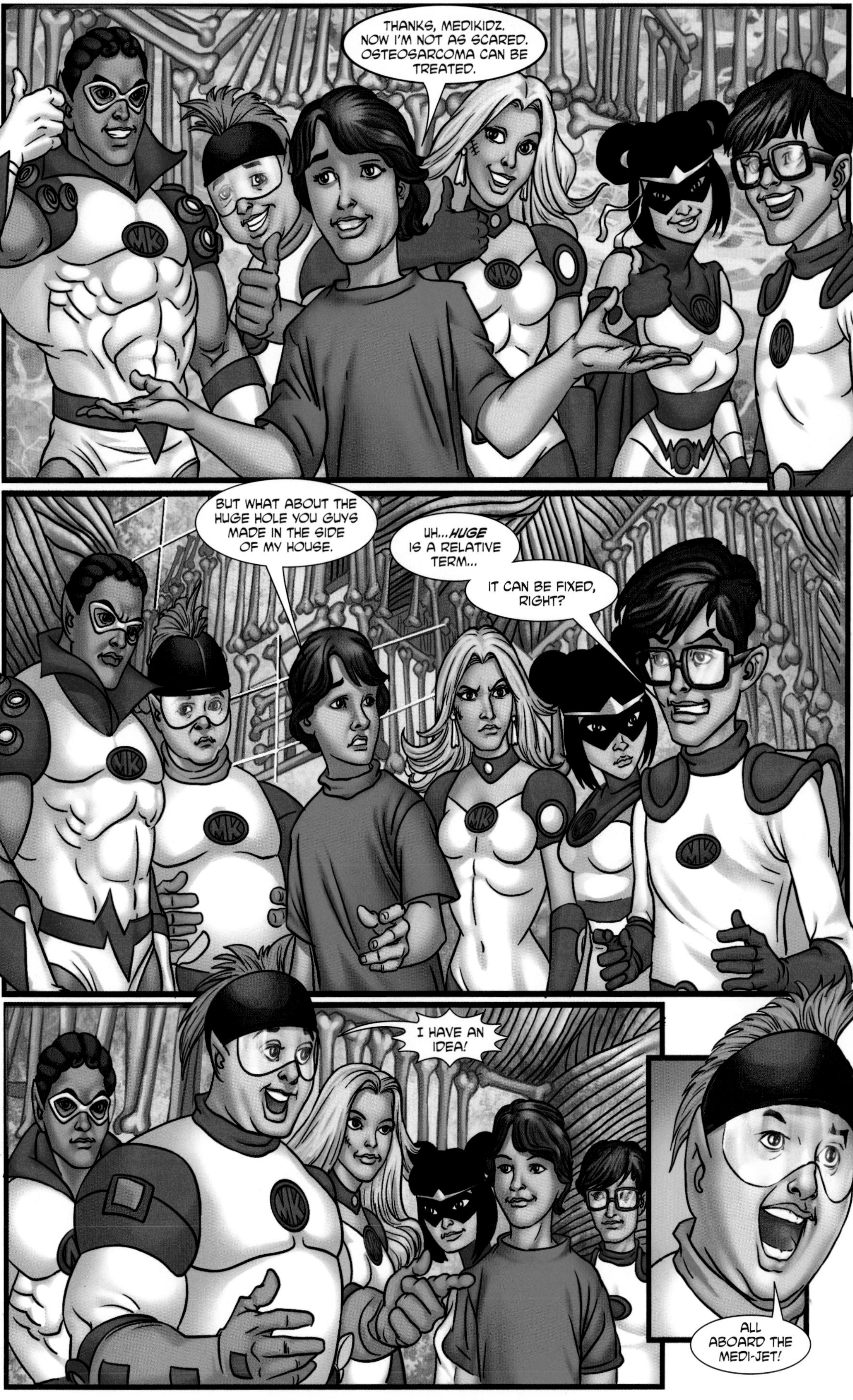
THANKS, MEDIKIDZ. NOW I'M NOT AS SCARED. OSTEOSARCOMA CAN BE TREATED.
BUT WHAT ABOUT THE HUGE HOLE YOU GUYS MADE IN THE SIDE OF MY HOUSE.
UH... *HUGE* IS A RELATIVE TERM...
IT CAN BE FIXED, RIGHT?
I HAVE AN IDEA!
ALL ABOARD THE MEDI-JET!

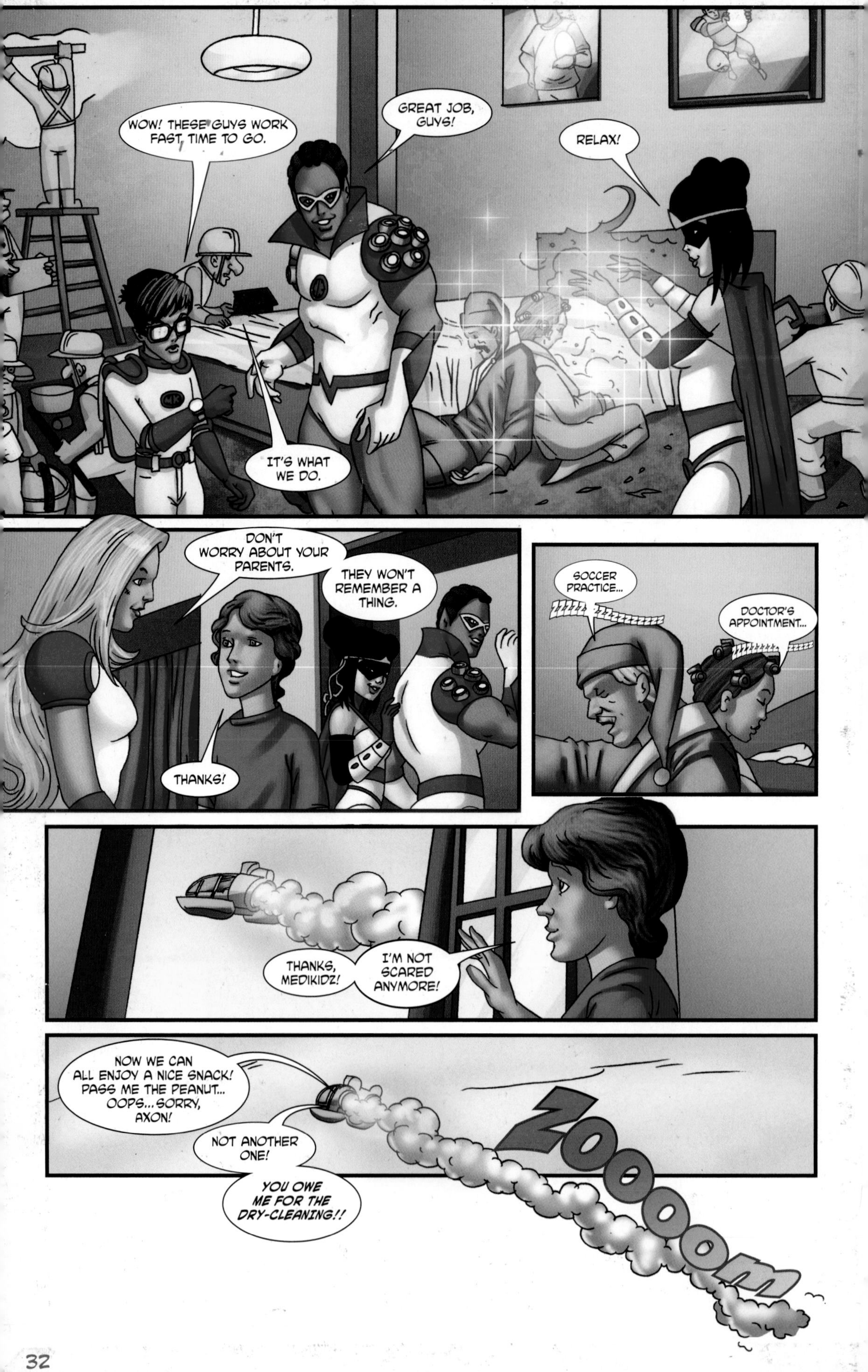
WOW! THESE GUYS WORK FAST. TIME TO GO.
GREAT JOB, GUYS!
RELAX!
IT'S WHAT WE DO.
DON'T WORRY ABOUT YOUR PARENTS.
THEY WON'T REMEMBER A THING.
THANKS!
SOCCER PRACTICE...
ZZZZZ ZZZZZZZZZZZ
DOCTOR'S APPOINTMENT...
THANKS, MEDIKIDZ!
I'M NOT SCARED ANYMORE!
NOW WE CAN ALL ENJOY A NICE SNACK! PASS ME THE PEANUT... OOPS... SORRY, AXON!
NOT ANOTHER ONE!
YOU OWE ME FOR THE DRY-CLEANING!!
ZOOOOOM